Being Here
Is Glorious

Being Here
Is Glorious

On Rilke, Poetry, and Philosophy

✦

With a new translation
of the *Duino Elegies*

James D. Reid

NORTHWESTERN UNIVERSITY PRESS
EVANSTON, ILLINOIS

Northwestern University Press
www.nupress.northwestern.edu

Printed in the United States of America

10   9   8   7   6   5   4   3   2   1

Library of Congress Cataloging-in-Publication Data

Reid, James D. (James David), author.
    Being here is glorious : on Rilke, poetry, and philosophy : with a new
translation of the Duino Elegies / James D. Reid.
        pages cm.
    Includes index.
    ISBN 978-0-8101-3134-7 (cloth : alk. paper) — ISBN 978-0-8101-3135-4
(pbk. : alk. paper)
    1. Rilke, Rainer Maria, 1875–1926. Duineser Elegien. 2. Rilke, Rainer Maria,
1875–1926—Criticism and interpretation. 3. Philosophy in literature. I. Rilke,
Rainer Maria, 1875–1926. Duineser Elegien. English. II. Title.
    PT2635.I65D8135 2015
    831.912—dc23

                                                                2015017545

For Candace Craig and Rick Furtak

CONTENTS

ACKNOWLEDGMENTS

As short as it is, this book has been a long time coming; and there are many people, too many to name here, who deserve thanks.

I'd like to be able to say that the project has been properly gestating, and that the finished version couldn't have arrived any earlier than it has, according to some strict and unalterable law of creative movement. But I know the tricks of *Fortuna* far too well, and the accidents that interrupt our labors and protract them unseasonably, and the chances and occasions that sometimes make for a better project than what we originally had in mind. It came out when it could, but only as all things with or without miraculous intervention do, and often against our expectations. Accidents should be gratefully acknowledged from time to time—happy things sometimes fall.

My interest in Rilke reaches back into my early years as an undergraduate student of physics, chemistry, biology, and philosophy, with a passion for literature and poetry, and an interest in how so many conflicting interests might be reconciled with one another. That philosophy won out should not sound surprising to anyone deeply conversant with what philosophy in its comprehensive designs at least attempts to do, despite the philosophers' chronic inability to reach anything like the consensus scientists rightly expect in their own disciplines. Nor should it strike as odd those who come to philosophy from other disciplines, as dissatisfied specialized inquirers and lovers of a human knowledge tied to human interest and what Heidegger frequently calls *das Seiende im Ganzen*— and what the Greeks named, more simply, *ta polla*—often do.

I began work on the translation of the *Duino Elegies* in 2007, and found myself still revising and expanding a lengthy philosophical introduction to Rilke's poetry in the early months of 2014. The first version of both the translation and the philosophical interpretation, which was initially one continuous essay, was completed in the early months of 2009 and readied for publication shortly thereafter for the University of Scranton Press (now defunct). The manuscript remained essentially unchanged until January 2014, when I was encouraged to expand some of the introductory material and decided, in consequence of the revision work, to rethink the structure of the book, for Northwestern University Press. I won't say that I understand Rilke, philosophy, Plato, Platonism, and poetry better now than I did seven years ago, when this book was conceived, or that I'm better placed to translate Rilke today. But I can say that recent invitations from outside quarters to revisit the work's argument have led to more nuanced conceptions, or a better presentation, of what Rilke was trying to do in the *Duino Elegies*, and why Plato should matter to anyone interested in Rilke's poetry, and in poetry more generally, from a philosophical perspective. It is always possible, if not always useful, to wonder whether one's more youthful vision captured more adequately, and before others began to comment upon one's work, what one originally (thought one) had to say. But I'm pleased with the result of my attempts to respond to so many helpful comments and critical suggestions in both the early stages of the manuscript's planning and development and in the final stretch of revision. Apologies in advance if I've forgotten to mention anyone who believes he or she had some role in making this project possible.

Thanks are due, first, to Chin-Tai Kim (Case Western Reserve University) for introducing me to philosophy and its history—in the West and in the East—and, just as importantly, for showing me the importance of philosophy in almost every sense in which philosophy can be said to matter, or has come to matter to me (that I have nothing more to say on this score is an index of his importance to my own development). Next, at least in the order of time, thanks to David Kaetzel, with whom I worked closely on biological problems for a number of years and published a few articles in molecular biology; who encouraged me to take up a career in the hard sciences; and who often used to wonder why anyone interested in the molecular mechanisms of carcinogenesis and the Loop-III region of platelet-derived growth factor (PDGF) A-chain would spend, or waste, his lunch hours pouring over Homer's *Iliad* or Hegel's *Phenomenology*. I thank David for provoking me to defend the loves of a humanist in the face of well-meant opposition from the philanthropic biochemist's beliefs about the prospect of reducing human suffering by scientific means, and for generously allowing me to spend long hours away from the lab to study German and philosophy with Daniel Breazeale and Ronald Bruzina—both important influences on my earliest days of philosophic inquiry (thanks to Dan and Ron, too)—on another part of the University of Kentucky's campus, far removed, in more ways than one, from the Medical School and the corridors of the Department of Pharmacology. I'm sure David would be surprised to find himself mentioned here, if he ever discovers this book. In response to his pertinent questions and persistent perplexity I have nothing better to say today than what I said almost twenty years ago, although I think I understand my youthful response more fully now than I did back then: the larger human problems endure, despite the progress our sciences sometimes make. The choice in favor of philosophy has in any event been made and, barring dementia, irrevocably.

My love of this particular poet would not have taken shape as a project in recent years without the encouragement of Rick Anthony Furtak, Jeff Gainey, and Henry Carrigan. To Rick I'm grateful for conversations on Rilke, philosophy, and related matters from which I've profited more than I can convey, for more years than I care to count, for his own work on issues I take to be central to philosophy's (Platonic) concern, and for help-ful comments on a draft of the interpretive essay and the translation of the *Elegies* (here, too, the brevity of the expression of thanks is in inverse proportion to the significance of the individual in the author's life and work). Thanks to Jeff for his interest in my work from its official begin-ning, for his unflagging patience and excitement as the manuscript neared completion, and for his final willingness to inform me about Scranton's unfortunate decision to close its press, when other members of the Scran-ton community took silence and avoidance for wisdom (that he wasn't able to take final editorial credit for the appearance of this volume is no fault of his own). And thanks to Henry for seeing this project through to publishable completion, for several conversations about what the vol-ume should include, and for standing behind a work, with patience and unfeigned zeal, that some editors might have found difficult to place, but that Henry understood and appreciated and encouraged at every step of the way.

I'd also like to thank two anonymous reviewers for the Northwestern University Press, both of whom provided encouraging words and helpful comments on the penultimate draft of the translation and philosophical reflections, and one of whom prodded me to share here a slightly more nuanced interpretation of what, for the sake of abbreviation, we can call Plato's stance on poetry and the poetic endeavor, more consistent with the richness of the Platonic achievement, and in keeping with my own consid-ered views on Plato's ambiguities and the fruitful tensions the dialogues often display facing mimetic poetry and the poetic statement. The result of my efforts to satisfy the second referee is, I think, a stronger defense of the philosophical importance of poetry than the original manuscript had to offer.

My gratitude also extends to my former advisers Michael Forster and Charles Larmore—both formerly of the University of Chicago, the latter now at Brown, the former presently an Alexander von Humboldt Profes-sor at the University of Bonn—for encouraging me to bring this work to completion, when I was still a former student struggling to find his way in the philosophical profession and seeking professional advice, and for encouraging me from early on to write about the issues I found myself caring about in my own, at times eccentric, way. Forster's own work on Herder and German philosophy of language and hermeneutics is a testament to his commitment to philosophical modes of writing that don't readily conform to the dryness that characterizes most of what appears in the Anglo-American philosophical world. Larmore's short but illuminating book on the philosophical significance of Romanticism has accompanied my work in philosophy, poetry, and literature for many years.

Martha Nussbaum's seminar on Aristotle and Kant and theories of virtue at the University of Chicago in 1998, as well as her own published contributions to philosophy and literature, also played an important role in the development of views that found their way into the present book (my published essay on Kant, "Morality and Sensibility in Kant: Toward a Theory of Virtue," bears evidence of her influence). Robert Pippin is someone whose work I've lived with for almost as long as I've considered myself an aspiring philosopher. Given what I think I know about both Hegel and Pippin's Hegel and about Pippin's own views on many things related to topics addressed in the present volume, I don't doubt that Robert would find many reasons to quarrel with several of the claims I try to defend in what follows.

I began the work of translation in Denver in unsettled circumstances, and finished a first draft of the *Elegies* in a lovely cottage in the woods in Williamsburg, Virginia, while teaching in an unusually quiet and hospitable environment at the College of William and Mary. Thanks to my colleagues in the Department of Philosophy at the College for their support (especially Mike Cole and Matthew Haug for many evenings shooting pool); to Patricia Kandle for providing the cabin, great food, good conversation, and an undistracted atmosphere when it came time to work; and to Tom, who sometimes oversaw the work in progress on the deck, not knowing what precisely he observed—the Thoreauvian temptations of the forest and "brute neighbors" and the solitude Rilke and Thoreau both prized were never stronger.

Thanks are also due to Clifford J. Naylor for exceptional work on the indexes, and for the last-minute discovery of several typographical mistakes; to Preston Brasch for meticulous transcription work; and to Eleanor Anderson for a lovely woodcut-like image of the catkins I'd hoped several years ago to find hanging on the cover; to Ella Street, for introducing me to Preston and Eleanor, for inspiring conversations touching on matters broached in the philosophical essays, for reminding me of the importance of Tocqueville and the political dimension of the problems my work as a whole addresses, and, more recently, for editorial advice rooted in a close and careful reading of the manuscript in the weeks leading up to its submission—her friendship, still in the making and always fruitfully troubled, has proved itself invaluable to me (*Wie hab ich das gefühlt was Abschied heißt*). Thanks to my parents, Mary and David Babuder, for an unexpected copy of Rilke's *Gesammelte Werke in fünf Bänden*, and for asking often how the work was coming along. Thanks to James Carey (St. John's College, Santa Fe, and the United States Air Force Academy), meticulous scholar and thoughtful reader of everything he touches, for helpful comments on an early draft of the manuscript, and for inviting me to reinstate the commas in the first line of the "First Elegy." Thanks to my former colleagues at the United States Air Force Academy, especially Colonel James Cook (who had the enviable opportunity to meet Gadamer at Heidelberg while he was a graduate student studying philosophy abroad), Carl Ficarrotta (now a visiting scholar at the University of North Carolina, Chapel Hill) for tolerating, and in some cases encouraging, my frequent use of ADL to complete a first draft of the philosophical essays, and Will Caudill for keeping things interesting with a wit worthy of Sir John Falstaff. Thanks to Coralie, endlessly provocative, for a few good thoughts about a few important things; to Butternut and Tumbleweed, two more brute neighbors who helped in a few small but important ways; and to K. (not Joseph), the happy thing who fell before I began, but who remained in mind from beginning to end, and was especially present as I approached the final stanza of the "Tenth Elegy."

Thanks, finally but just as importantly, to Candace R. Craig, for her long-standing love of Rilke, captured in a youthful essay of her own on the *Elegies* (titled, appropriately enough, "The Birth of Music out of the Spirit of Tragedy"), for comments on several passages of translation and argument still in the making, for much that makes work of this sort possible, including leaving me alone when it seemed fitting to work elsewhere, for formatting the manuscript for publication with meticulous attention to detail and enviable technical skill, and for wanting this book to appear almost as much as its author, against the daily obstacles and the many reasons we offer, against our better judgment, to defer.

I dedicate this volume to Candace and to Rick.

Being Here
Is Glorious

INTRODUCTION

The need to introduce a book with a few orienting remarks easily gives way to apology. It would be more convenient or modest to leave the reader alone with the work, and a mistake to try to work out too much in advance—anticipating possible objections, alternative positions, and conflicting approaches. As Hegel wisely reminds us, it is impossible to avoid dogmatizing in a *Vorwort*, paying injustice to significant others, friends and foes alike, and flouting the proper, fully executed form of truth.[1]

But the reader deserves to know in advance something of what the author intends, where his work fits in with other works of its kind, or why it fails to fall in with certain readily identifiable genres, and why he saw fit to impose himself upon the reading public. A few introductory remarks are consequently in order, touching on (1) questions of style, in light of the book's aim, (2) matters pertaining to translation, and (3) the philosophical issues the author means to address and the methods to be employed or avoided, as the case may be.

On Style

> Poetry is going to be as rational as it *can* be, and reason as passionate as it *may*.[2]

If the book the reader has in hand can be said to have a thesis, it might be said to run: there is poetry in good philosophy and philosophy in some great poetry, and that is as it should be. What remains, then, is to catch up with this proposition, and to flesh out what it means and implies, by considering exemplary cases of poetry and philosophy that include both.

My aim in the interpretive essays is to begin an argument for the philosophical importance of poetry in general and Rilke's *Duino Elegies* in particular, with Platonic objections and concerns and a few modern variants chiefly in mind, and with Rilke's poetic achievement, and the translation work that follows, more or less continuously in view. In light of Rilke's youthful enthusiasm for Nietzsche, and given the poet's influence upon several important European philosophers, including Martin Heidegger, this may seem to be a superfluous ambition. But it remains the case that poets are not always thought to think, certainly not in ways that invite fruitful comparison with what professional philosophers do. Even Heidegger, otherwise well disposed toward poetry as a thoughtful response to the human condition and attentive to Rilke's poetic vocabulary and the coherence of the poet's basic stance,[3] measured what he took to be Rilke's metaphysics and found it wanting. As the reader who gets beyond these preliminaries will see, I take seriously Rilke's contribution to the history of thought, responsive at its very best to the difficulties of being human, although in form, if not in substance, the *Duino Elegies* is clearly no *Critique of Pure Reason*.

As both a lover of poetry and a professional philosopher, I am aware of the difficulties inherent in such an enterprise, where the task, at least in part, is to do *stylistic* justice to both poetry and philosophy. The poet often rebels against the tendency toward prosaic statement, which cannot keep pace with poetic enthusiasm and suggestiveness, and often seems an impoverished recasting of what should be allowed to stand on its own feet, or better to run. I often write, surrendering to the poet's influence, without the convenient "in what follows I intend to prove that . . ." in part because I'm not sure that I can prove all that much (I'm not sure that philosophers manage to do anything more than suggest and argue, and ever fall short of strict proof), but also because, relatedly, I take the origins of philosophical argument and proof to be matters of vision rather than argument. But the philosopher, at least in the Socratic vein, is moved to interpret and to argue, and is commonly uncomfortable with murkiness in argumentation and conspicuous gaps in the account.

I'm not quite convinced by the author of *Beyond Good and Evil* that every great philosophy is "the personal confession of its author and a kind of involuntary and unconscious memoir."[4] Or that philosophy is only this. Plato's Socrates sometimes claims that he's not considering detached views and arguments but persons. But he often avers that it doesn't matter whose argument is under scrutiny, that the logos alone is what needs examining.[5] I don't think this is an instance of Plato's carelessness or confusion, but an important indication of what the philosophic endeavor amounts to at its best: earnest self-examination cannot be cleanly divorced from reflection upon the *logoi* that take up residence in the soul, even if someone's *logoi* give voice to the less logical or discursive features of the author's personality—modes of perceiving, scope and structure of the imagination, emotions, moods, and the traits of enduring character.

A book of this sort is really the product of two distinct attitudes toward the world of human thought and speech, each often suspicious of the other, and consequently difficult to reconcile. It is with a reconciling aim that the interpretive essays were written, in the spirit of Plato's accomplishment in the dialogues, which artfully combine philosophy and poetry in a puzzling way that invites us to consider the nature of both. And the style of the prose is meant to appeal to persons enamored with poetry and attuned to the importance of discursive thought.

The translation of the *Elegies* that follows the interpretive material is an essential part of the work, and could with some justification be placed first, as it came in the order of composition, as provocation of the philosophical interpretation of the poetry. It has been my working conviction throughout that our thoughts cannot be cleanly divorced from the words we choose to express what we think about the most important things. *How* we name things and go on to speak of them is a measure of the quality of our thought, beyond the otherwise laudable attempts to achieve precision in our definitions of certain basic concepts, and before we deploy the philosophical arguments we hope will convince imagined interlocutors.

The *Duino Elegies* are obviously a cycle of *poems*. It matters that the poet chose to express his sense of the human condition and its enduring problems in verse. While some of the thoughts expressed in the *Elegies* have their prosaic counterparts, in the poet's correspondence and essays, for instance, it is their poetic embodiment that matters chiefly here, in keeping with the view that some truths come home initially in the poem, before philosophers enter the hermeneutic scene. A few words, then, on the translation that follows the philosophical material.

On Translation

In some sophisticated circles it is no longer plausible to speak of literalness as the translator's aim, although it isn't always clear what the alternative should be. We are now more sensitive to the metaphorical dimension of the most literal speech, and—for some of us thanks partly to Nietzsche—tend to see in the literal meaning of a word a trope or metaphor that's passed into common circulation at the expense of its figurative origins.

But in practice this philosophical stance is often irrelevant to the translator's work. An *Engel* is an angel, after all, and a *Tier* is an animal. *Bleiben* and *remaining* both need interpreting. If words invite interpretation and analysis, it hardly matters whether the tongue is German or English. The world doesn't speak German, but it isn't the Englishman's possession either. Everything said invites another saying. The translator's work is simply to make a poem that emulates its original, and that conveys what the author takes to be his chosen poet's vision and meaning—an uninformative statement of purpose, perhaps, but one that at least captures in the abstract what I take myself to have been trying to do. Some truisms become truer, or show their usefulness beyond the palaver, in light of certain failures to live up to what often appears obvious.

I have tried to produce a version of the *Duineser Elegien* in English that preserves the sense of the original as well as the rhythm and length of each line, and with a fluency comparable to the German. A translation that fails to embody both the matter *and* the form of the original in the target language fails, in my view, to offer a sincere attempt at translation, unless a case can be made that the content of a poetic work can be detached from its form. Although it is fair to say that "ideas seem to take the lead" over formal constraint in the free stanzas of the *Elegies*, in contrast with the *Sonnets to Orpheus*, as Rick Anthony Furtak notes in the introduction to his translation of the *Sonnets*, the poems translated below have a distinctive sound and movement, and a musical quality of their own, that the translator should respect and aspire to realize in his own tongue.[6]

As for the translation of Rilke's carefully chosen words, I generally prefer Anglo-Saxon equivalents, where this is possible, without sacrificing the musical quality of the original. So, for instance, I translate "Dasein" as "being" rather than "existence"—in part because it sounds better, at least in my ear, in part because "existence" carries connotations, especially in some strands of the existentialist tradition, that I've come to think are foreign to Rilke. Or, to take another example, puzzled over by Gass in *Reading Rilke*, I translate the well-known opening lines of the "First Elegy," *Wer, wenn ich schriee, hörte mich denn aus der Engel / Ordnungen*: "Who, if I cried out, would hear me among the angels' / orders." Mitchell, whose version of the *Elegies* is still among the best, or at least the one against which I've repeatedly measured my own efforts, offers "hierarchies"—perhaps echoing MacIntyre—for *Ordnungen*, although Rilke's angelic realm is not so clearly arrayed and defined as the language of hierarchies suggests and, as I hope to show below, there is good reason to think that Rilke's angels stand *beneath* us. Cohn's "ranked Angels" is an odd choice, or so it strikes the ear of someone who spent two years teaching at a military academy and who knows something of Rilke's own aversions to military speech. Rilke's *Ordnungen* are territories, regions, or domains of being; so Gass's "Dominions" seems preferable.[7] Boney's "angelic hosts" strikes a perhaps unintended biblical note, which I've tried to avoid (most scholars agree that Rilke's angels are not best interpreted in light of the Christian tradition). And Leishman, whose version of the opening lines I otherwise prefer, expands the *Engel* into the "angelic" and, I think, distorts both the rhythm and the individualizing sense of the German.

Two more examples, with Mitchell's rendition exclusively in mind: the first three lines of the second stanza of the "Sixth Elegy" run in German: *Wir aber verweilen, / ach, uns rühmt es zu blühn, und ins verspäte Innre / unserer endlichen Frucht gehn wir verraten hinein.* Mitchell expands the first line with a "still" ("But *we* still linger, alas") and renders the simple, compact "uns rühmt es zu blühn" "we, whose pride is in blossoming," when he might have said "we who glory in blooming." Again, in the "Ninth Elegy," Mitchell adds an unnecessary "completely" to "But to have been / just *once* . . ." and expands the suggestive "to have been *earthly*" (my rendering of "*irdisch* gewesen zu sein") into the semantically narrowed and metrically overburdened "to have been at one with the earth . . . ."

One could multiply examples endlessly. I certainly don't wish to leave the reader with the impression that I know better, in every case, how to translate a poet as demanding as Rilke. As Stephen Spender remarks in the translator's introduction to his felicitous rendition of Rilke's *Marien-Leben*, translation is ever a matter of compromise. And as Mark Harman observes, "Rilke both invites and resists translation."[8] Dissatisfaction with existing translations is often one of the principal reasons for attempting one's own. But as Harman also notes in the same context, and in a way that comes closer to the motives that inspired the present work, there is something about Rilke's voice that invites the reader to think of Rilke's production as though it were written for each of us directly and alone.

This, by itself, can be a strong incentive to work through the poet's vision for oneself, and to render a version of one's favorite cycle in one's own tongue. But we translate always with other translations in mind, or in the ear. I've benefited enormously from the work of all those predecessors, twenty or more in all, if Harman's reckoning is accurate, who risked the attempt to carry the *Elegies* over into pregnant and often mellifluous English, despite my criticisms of a few of the better-known versions. It is perhaps enough to say: my task throughout was to carry over the sense of the poems into musical English, in opposition to a tendency, even among the better translators, to produce what I sometimes perceive to be stilted versions of the *Elegies*, with lines swelling in English beyond their limits in the original, and often obscuring or constricting what I take to be their sense. At some point, one has to resign oneself to what everyone knows: translation is always interpretation, and the product of the translator's work is a new and imperfect thing. Eventually, in face of the awful brevity of life, one has to pronounce the work finished and allow it to be.

On Rilke, Poetry, Plato, and Philosophy

A final word about the interpretive and philosophical material, if only to help the more philosophically inclined reader appreciate the aim, scope, and structure of the philosophical discussion, but also to caution the philologist and historicist and the biographically attuned interpreter of Rilke not to expect more, or to hope for something else, than what I intend in what follows.

As earlier readers of the manuscript were quick to recognize, there are two principal items on its agenda, which may at first blush appear unrelated. (For the convenience of the reader, I have parceled out the discussion and the translation into two parts, and divided the first part into a prelude and three chapters. Readers uninterested in Plato, Platonism, and the quarrel between the philosopher and the poet in Plato's dialogues, but curious about what I have to say about Rilke and the poems, may easily skip to the third chapter of part 1. Readers who wish to begin with the *Duino Elegies* are invited to open to part 2, and to explore the more philosophical portions of the work subsequently, if what they find in the poems moves them to delve into the philosophical essays.)

On the one hand, the essays in part 1 mean to provoke discussion about a long-standing philosophical bias against the poetic statement initiated by Plato or, to be more precise, by the figure of Socrates who plays such a commanding role in the dialogues. Indications of dissatisfaction with what poets do or say are discernible in the fragments of Xenophanes—himself a poet, writing in the very epic meter used by the poets he attacks—and Heraclitus as well, who famously claimed that Homer and Archilochus deserve to be beaten with a stick. But the attack upon poetry in the Platonic dialogues is the most thorough to be found in the ancient Greek world. In any event, philosophical hostility to poetry goes back a long way, and includes poets whose work includes a philosophical dimension and philosophers, like Parmenides, who chose to write in verse.

It might, therefore, appear that Rilke isn't much at issue in the first third or so of the manuscript, but this would be a mistaken impression. I move slowly toward Rilke's own work precisely because I intend to situate the *Elegies* in a philosophical setting that mainstream students and translators of Rilke may not be likely to take seriously in their own work with the poems, but also, and just as importantly, because I'd like to convince a few like-minded philosophers who don't read much Rilke that they should. I hope to convince the reader in those parts of what follows that deal more abstractly with issues I take to be germane to Rilke's own poetic labors that poetry and philosophy are neighbors, and neighbors sometimes engaged in a similar quest who ought to recognize the value of each other's efforts and achievements.

On the other hand, the essays aim to shed light on the significance and to argue for the enduring value of Rilke's contribution to a problem that has stirred some of the more important philosophers in the European tradition right from the very start. I include Plato and his successors here, and read the dialogues as contributions to moral philosophy or ethics, broadly construed. But the problem I intend to probe also finds a thought-provoking response in the work of philosophically dissident figures like Pascal, Hamann, and Jacobi in the early modern era, and in the writings of more recent thinkers like Kierkegaard, Nietzsche, Heidegger, and, more recently still, Stanley Cavell—namely: how, and on what basis, we might find life to be significant, valuable, and worth affirming in light of the many reasons to be dissatisfied, perplexed, and skeptical about the value of the world in which we find ourselves cast.

This strand, or question, deserves to be called *seminal* for the current project, as it motivates the reckoning with Plato and the Platonic legacy, as well as the work of translation, and the engagement with Rilke's *Elegies* and the poet's intellectual and poetic preoccupations throughout his productive life.

Both strands of the interpretive essays are essential to the book's overall design, although it can sometimes appear, especially to the more philosophically oriented reader, that the issues broached in the opening pages are left to the side, as the discussion advances into the more patently Rilkean territory of the *Elegies*. For it strikes me that contemporary ethics and moral philosophy too often share the Platonic assumption that moral reasoning and argument, and reflection upon the nature of both, can be cleanly and happily divorced from serious engagement with poetic discourse, and that this is one among several reasons why Rilke has not played a prominent part in the work of contemporary moral, social, and political thinkers grappling with what Nietzsche called the problem of nihilism.

The Platonic attack on the poetic statement's claim to truth has had a decisive impact on the course of Western aesthetics, for better or for worse. Kant's views on aesthetic judgment, at least in parts of the third *Critique*, inherit in a modern guise the Platonic assumption that judgments pertaining to the beautiful in art tell us more about our own state of mind, and less about the object we associate with the experience.[9] And no less an art critic and philosopher of art than Arthur Danto suggested that Plato set the agenda for the history of that branch of philosophy that, since Baumgarten, has come to be known as aesthetics. Hegel's view, to take an additional weighty instance, is both Platonic and anti-Platonic, for reasons it would be worth spelling out in another context.[10] There are more stances on this issue than I can possibly canvass in what follows. But there is a decidedly Platonic criticism of the arts, and poetry in particular, on what we might call epistemological and metaphysical, if not always moral, grounds that continues today; and a view about art and poetry as estranged from the truth that some are likely to assume, without Plato and his successors in view.

We would do well, then, to consider the Platonic bias, and to evaluate its merits in light of our own contemporary concerns and insights, if only to understand what prompted philosophical hostility to poetry in the earliest stages of the history of philosophy. We may not share some of the views that come forward in the Platonic dialogues, but still import Platonic concepts into our own sense of what poets mean to do, even when we resist the lure of what some philosophers in search of truth outside of physics and neurobiology are wont to call "scientism." As John Lysaker wisely notes in an important study of poetry and philosophy, building upon insights developed by Martin Heidegger, we often confront poetic texts with categories—symbol, metaphor, and allegory, for instance—that risk "a kind of Platonism, one that idealizes content and renders form in terms of sensual arrangements."[11] Platonic conceptions are often at work in the interpretation of poetry without our being fully aware of the questionable metaphysical sources of the frameworks we take for granted as natural. We may be resolutely "this-worldly" but still find ourselves wedded to conceptual frameworks that owe their origins to strands of thought that cut against the grain of our more worldly interpretations and affirmations of artistic endeavor.[12]

But focusing on Platonism is also crucial because it is Plato himself who shows us why poetry should matter to philosophy, even when the philosopher is taken to be the poet's superior or adversary. Plato's work often displays the very poetic qualities one or more of his characters in the dialogues discover reasons to disavow. And some of the dialogues give evidence of the value of poetic discourse itself in the development of the human soul, if only to help the pupil discover in the long run what Socrates in the *Republic* calls "the beauty of reason."[13]

Plato or Platonism is additionally important in the work that follows because, from the other side, Rilke's *Elegies* themselves are responsive to what we can call, I think fairly, the Platonic aspiration to transcendence, rooted in dissatisfaction with the apparent transience or ephemerality of all things and the unsettling fact of death, which both Socrates in the Platonic dialogues and Rilke in the *Elegies* place at the center of the human problem. In a way that I hope will become clear in what follows, Rilke's final affirmative stance in the *Elegies* comes close to embodying something of the Platonic aspiration to overcome the fleeting world of human experience in the "eternal" spaces of the poem. Like Proust, on some readings,[14] Rilke can be read as offering a questionable aesthetic or metaphysical solution to problems we often associate with ethical life.

My argument, then, runs toward the conclusion that Rilke's poetry is responsive to Platonic problems in a way that poses a serious threat to certain Platonic aspirations; that Rilke's poetry also embodies something of the Platonic aspiration still; and that Plato's own work gives evidence of the poet's lasting role in lending significance to life.

The importance of this statement of purpose, or where the argument means to lead, and the methodological limits it imposes upon the present study, cannot be overestimated, especially in light of the many reasons scholars and intellectual historians discover to approach Rilke, and the diverse methods of inquiry students of Rilke employ to shed light on the poems. If I'd meant to offer scholarly contributions to the literature on Rilke's social setting, for instance, or the biographical details that may shed light on the *Elegies*, or the specific lines of influence that can be traced to Rilke and beyond our poet, or to provide evidence that Rilke's poetry embodies some more recent view on poetics among contemporary critics, or deviates from contemporary literary theory in some interesting way, my argument should be judged a failure. This is a work that roots itself in philosophy and that treats nonphilosophical sources of insight as instruments and means toward the goal of understanding and interpreting Rilke's possible contribution to the philosophical conversation initiated by Socrates, Plato, and their predecessors and carried forward in more recent thinkers. There are many fine studies of Rilke from literary critical, historical, and biographical points of view (the *Cambridge Companion to Rilke* is a useful example), but the present volume is not meant to compete with volumes of this sort.

But the reader should be forewarned further: the views that surface in Plato's dialogues are far more complicated and conflicted than a work of this size and scope can possibly address fairly, and with the thoroughness that an author of Plato's subtlety and comprehensiveness demands. My short remarks on the *Ion* are meant to provoke and to motivate, and not to offer a scholarly contribution to this still rather neglected dialogue.

I decided right from the start that I did not want to write a series of philosophical essays that would overshadow the *Elegies* themselves, and confine the translation of Rilke's great poetic cycle to an appendix of sorts, as though the poems were meant merely to illustrate a philosophical thesis to be defended on its own. And so I open the interpretive material with the *Ion* because this short dialogue, the shortest, in fact, of the extant dialogues, condenses anxieties that show up throughout the Platonic corpus (about a dozen Platonic dialogues deal with the problem of poetry, at least by some reckonings), anticipating views that come forward in the much longer discussion of poetry in the *Republic*, and takes aim at a target that resembles in the current scene those of us who look to poetic texts as fountains of insight into the human condition. It stands, then, as a compelling attack upon the sort of poetic criticism a few of us philosophically minded readers of poetry practice. Whether the views that come forward in this dialogue, and others I consider, are Plato's own I leave to historians of philosophy and philologists to consider. In legal settings, questions of intent are often decisive; in philosophical and literary affairs, I'm not so sure.[15]

When I speak of "Platonism" as poetry's adversary, then, I do not mean to minimize the oft-conflicted nature of the vision that finds expression in the Platonic corpus, but to single out a few threads among many that find a place in Plato's work that certain figures in the tradition (Plotinus comes to mind), including some philologists and historical scholars of the Platonic dialogues, have isolated and often exaggerated.[16] In some ways, the author of the *Republic* is something of an ally, to the extent that he writes in a poetic vein, and insofar as one of his characters construes the good, or what we might call the realm or the source of our values, to be implicated in any reasonable sense and account of what exists. It should in any case go almost without saying that Plato ranks among the world's greatest literary and *poetic* authors. And *that* is a problem the lover of wisdom should be more inclined to make his own.

Part One

✦

Interpreting

Prelude

Affirmation and opinionativeness are express signs of stupidity.
—Montaigne, "Of Experience" (*Essays* III.20)

The official task of an interpretive *introduction*, as the word itself suggests, is to lead the reader into the work, on the common assumption, I suppose, that the writer knows better than his readers what the work—in this case a cycle of poems and a body of philosophical writings on poetry and its aftermath—is about, or that the work cannot stand on its own, but must be placed, perhaps in certain social or political or intellectual circumstances, or that the author or translator possesses some key, metaphysical or psychological or otherwise, that will unlock some of its mysteries, and remove in advance the reader's anticipated doubts and uncertainties. An introduction is often meant to be reassuring, to situate something initially strange in a familiar setting, a dogmatic affair.

But an introduction can also be a way of leading the reader into strange landscapes, and inviting her to find her own way. A host introduces a guest speaker, not knowing what will be delivered and how it will strike the audience. Two strangers are introduced in the hope that they'll get along. An introduction can lead into obscurities and exacerbate uncertainties, and prompt the reader to wonder and, what amounts to the same thing in an ancient register, to begin to think. Sometimes the best introductions do little more than remove a few obstacles that block understanding and otherwise get in the way.

If we speak of Rilke, poetry, philosophy, and the like in what follows, then ours is a prologue armed "not in confidence / Of author's pen." For it strikes me that we are no better placed to say, definitively, what these things are and how they relate to one another and, just as importantly, to the world, than anyone, anywhere has been, and not by accident. They are, like every large and important thing, suggestions and provocations merely, invitations to pursue some track or to be misled, perhaps, by trick of fancy, and *questions* from first to last. We approach our theme in the spirit of Shakespeare, interpreted famously with the help of Keats as "being in uncertainties, Mysteries, doubts, without any irritable reaching after fact."[1] Or in the spirit of Rilke's own letters to Kappus, the voice of which a fine recent translator of the *Letters to a Young Poet* describes as "by turns confident, self-questioning, concerned, self-absorbed, open-minded, didactic, genuine, and affected."[2]/There is certainty at least in this: if anyone tells you that he knows what poetry, philosophy, language, being, and so on are, then he's either lying or naive, and begging to be refuted/In the realm of what is or appears to be most important, nobody is chief among those who know. To believe otherwise is intellectually fatal. As William James somewhere observes, uncertainty is the source of life and hope.

But we are not necessarily at a loss. There is nowhere to begin but where others have spoken. We are acquainted with things at first by their names, and names often crystallize someone's argument and voice. To esteem charity and turning of the other cheek is to rehearse the stance of a carpenter's son. To praise the mind thinking and inquiring, rendering an account and ever alert, is to live in the shadow of Socrates. A plenary lecture on the metaphysics of harm is indebted, perhaps unwittingly, to ancient views on *ousia, pathos, aitia*.[3] We don't know what love is, or not quite as fully and richly what love might be, without the help of Dante or Shakespeare. Or what corrosive cynicism can mean and imply as well. We are begun by others, and remain a conversation. Tradition gives us the material of our contemporary designs, and often reads our disorders better than we can interpret our miseries by ourselves. If the world could, *per impossible*, be stripped of everything that's been said about it, in praise or slandering or in the neutralizing frame of mind, the remainder would be precisely—nothing. Or at least nothing about which anyone could care. "The greatest genius is the most indebted man."[4] In relation to what's preceded us, we are still, again cribbing Emerson on Shakespeare, out of doors; and our best thoughts and most personal disagreements clothe themselves in borrowed robes.

Chapter 1

An Ancient Quarrel between
Philosophy and Poetry

AUDREY: I do not know what poetical is. Is it honest in deed and word? Is it a true thing?
TOUCHSTONE: No, truly; for the truest poetry is the most feigning.

—*As You Like It*

A Lesson from Plato's *Ion* with a Nod to the *Republic*

We begin, then, with an ancient story drawn from Plato that places our own endeavor to interpret poetry and to make a case for its importance in a questionable light, in order to provide fruitful friction for the subsequent defense of the philosophical importance of the poetic statement, or the importance of a certain philosophic openness to what great poets have to say, before we allow our chosen poet to help decide what our topics and arguments and interpretations of human life might be.

Socrates meets up with Ion of Ephesus, a rhapsode who's just returned from Epidaurus after a prize-winning recitation of Homeric poetry at the festival of Asclepius, puffed up and anxious to share with the philosopher his enthusiasm for the bard and his own interpretive art. The Socratic philosopher, so the story goes, is willing to flatter the lover of poetry, if only to put him at ease for the sake of conversation. But he seems not to be the sort of person to admire something he dimly understands, or to give his fullest assent to what calls for further explanation. If he's to share in Ion's excitement about his successful performance and the occasion of his poetic success, he must first endeavor to explain the nature and the source of poetry's charm, perhaps to get to the bottom of what the source poet, in this case Homer, and his followers *mean*—or at least to foreground the meaning or content of epic poetry, in opposition to its form. And, more importantly, to decide whether the lovers of poetry, and,

17

by implication, the poets themselves, really know things that others do not, or cannot, know.

Ion is eager to display his skill, and to illuminate the Homeric poems, revealing their unsurpassed excellence in telling sublime truth about war and peace, virtue and vice, the gods, Hades, death and punishment, salvation or glory, and other important things. (It is important to Socrates that Ion claims to be able to make sense of Homer, and not Hesiod and Archilochus as well.) Here, then, is the philosopher's chance to probe someone who claims to possess something like the wisdom he seeks, and to understand the nature of his own activity better.[1] And so they talk about the nature of poetry, or poetic inspiration, and its living interpretation in the rhapsode's performance, and the effects of both upon the audience, in what appears throughout a friendly exchange.

That Ion is a rhapsode and not a poet in his own right does not rule out the possibility that Plato means to explore the nature and limits of poetry in the dialogue, although, as Murdoch and others have pointed out, Socrates does not marshal a direct attack upon Homer and poetry, or poetic creativity and its product, in general, but limits his assault to "the secondary artist, the actor-critic."[2] The boundary between the reciter and his original was often fluid—epic poetry was originally an oral tradition: the rhapsode was expected to embellish, as Ion himself proudly claims,[3] and to correct his inherited original, with an eye on the poetic form of his recitation, and, in Ion's own case, to interpret the meaning of the poetry he's mastered (he serves as a judge or critic, *kritês*).[4] Homer and Hesiod are described elsewhere in the Platonic corpus as "wandering rhapsodes."[5] And in the framing narrative, Ion himself refers to the rhapsode's art as one among several "branches of music and poetry."[6] The dialogue itself quickly opens onto the larger question concerning the value of poetry's claim to truth, facing the craftsman's dependable expertise, and the sources of poetic wisdom. And the dialogue raises serious questions concerning the legitimacy of placing poems and the interpretation of poems at the center of one's intellectual and moral concern.[7] (A similar point is made, in a rather different context, in Socrates's playful interpretation of a poem by Simonides in the *Protagoras*, where Socrates notes, at the end of his sophistical endeavor, that "discussing poetry is much like attending the drinking parties of worthless and vulgar people." We ought, he goes on to say, to be willing to speak in our own voice, and not to hide behind another's words which, according to the *Phaedrus*, don't directly answer our most pressing questions, but simply repeat themselves endlessly, without commentary, amplification, argument, and defense.)[8] In any event, the dialogue raises serious questions and presents grave doubts about what the philosophically oriented reader of poetry hopes to gain from his labors, for reasons I mean to rehearse briefly here. Resuming the thread:

Before long, in a central stretch of the dialogue, the philosopher gets the rhapsode to admit that he's more like an inspired being than someone in the know, and chained to his favorite poet like an iron ring to a magnet, and infecting others with his enthusiasm when he recites and embellishes Homer (the suggestion, borne out by the remainder of the dialogue, is that the interpreter of Homer panders to the emotions and attachments of his audience); and the poet himself is like a man possessed and out of his wits, drawing milk and honey from ordinary rivers: "for a poet is a light and winged thing, and holy, and never able to compose until he's become inspired, and is beside himself, and reason and intelligence are no longer in him."[9] Lovers of poetry, and poets themselves, might well agree, interpreting the appeal to inspiration (literally "being filled with the god") as a mark of the poet's superiority to the everyday, unpoetic and uninspired frame of mind.[10] (Something like this view comes forward in the *Phaedrus*, where Socrates seems to praise divine madness as a source of insight. For a recent defense of poetic inspiration as essential to the work of writing poetry, see T. S. Eliot's *The Use of Poetry and the Use of Criticism*.)[11] But from the point of view developed by the ironic Socratic figure who appears in the *Ion*, and echoing a position Socrates brings forward in the *Apology*, the poet and his interpreters may utter many fine, elevated, and enchanting things, but it takes someone who truly *knows*, an artisan or a philosopher, to decide whether or not poetry has hit the mark of *truth*.

Much of the dialogue pursues the potential difference between what Homer says about various arts and crafts (*technai*), and what the true craftsman is able to say about both the content of his skill and the worth of the Homeric account. (This probably helps to account for Goethe's scornful dismissal of the dialogue as somehow beneath Plato, and certainly reinforces the poetically minded reader's suspicion that the *Ion* does not deal justly with the poet's work. Plato will try to do poetry greater justice in other contexts, including the *Republic*—which is still largely critical and unsympathetic—and in the *Symposium* and *Phaedrus*, where poetry and its representatives get a more charitable hearing.) If Homer or his disciple tells us something about medicine, for instance, it is the doctor, and not the rhapsode or, by implication, the poet himself—at least as poet—who's in the best position to decide the truth of the poet's dictum. Even if the poet has given voice to something true, he cannot *as a poet* be said to know the truth he's managed to convey; for knowing,

$(K) \rightarrow (K)$

by implication, involves being able to render an account of what you know. This is just what the poet cannot apparently do, at least without surrendering his poetic task and becoming philosophical or technical.[12] "Does it belong to the medical art or the rhapsode's," Socrates asks (rhetorically), "to properly diagnose whether Homer speaks correctly [about medical matters] or not?"[13] Where Homer speaks of chariot driving, it's the one who knows how to command the chariot who is best positioned to say whether the epic poet speaks well or ill. And so, too, facing all the other sorts of claims one finds in Homer and his interpreters. Eventually Socrates gets poor Ion to confess, or to agree, that his skill in interpreting Homer amounts, absurdly, to the art of generalship.

Even if the poet and his reciter possess a *technê* of some sort, it is an art or skill in presenting, or imitating, things about which the poet and the rhapsode remain ignorant.[14] But the dialogue's ironic praise of the poet and the rhapsode's inspiration places even this more modest claim— that the poet knows how to compose, or the rhapsode to speak, about certain things with genuine art, craft, or skill—in doubt. The *Ion* ends with Socrates praising the rhapsode's great beauty and divinity, but not his knowledge: "You're divine, but you don't praise Homer with the skill of a technician."[15]

There may be no true quarrel between the poet and the philosopher as the *Ion* would have it, at least by implication, provided that the poet, or his reciter, makes no claim to knowledge, technical or otherwise, but freely acknowledges that he speaks from *enthousiasmos* (enthusiasm, inspiration) and intends merely to inspire emotions similar to what he feels, or feigns (the dialogue suggests that the rhapsode traffics in artificially induced emotions), when he's reciting before his audience. Whether the poet intends to offer knowledge or not (the *Ion* leaves this an open question, I think), Plato's dialogue implies that the poet's *audience* often takes the poetic dictum for truth.[16] And to that extent the poet and his disciples deserve to be greeted by the philosophical and moral interpreter with a hearty dose of skepticism.

At best, then, and building upon, or drawing from, the more detailed and better known case against poetic endeavor developed in the *Republic*, poetry is a precursor to philosophy, a youthful stage in the development of the soul, and destined to be displaced by reason's apprehension of the truth about being, human nature, and the good.[17] At its worst, poetry delivers a spurious sense of knowledge, attaches us to things of little importance, and flatters those passions that obscure reason's insight.[18] Wisdom and the proper love of wisdom begin where poetry and divination and other dark utterances end. As Allan Bloom observes, the *Ion* depicts "the emergence of philosophy out of the [shadowy] world of [poetry and] myth."[19]

It can be difficult for the modern reader to sympathize with Plato's apparent hostility to poetry;[20] and this is only partly because many of us no longer understand what Plato (or Socrates) meant by philosophy as poetry's natural adversary in "an ancient quarrel" between the philosophers and the poets.[21] The difficulty stems more probably from our failure to understand how anyone, except for the most misguided moral fanatic and latter-day proponent of censorship, could make so much ado about something as innocuous as *art*, or why questions concerning beauty are often sidelined by the Platonic Socrates, in favor of metaphysical and epistemological, moral and political concerns. For Plato's conception of the poet's work and its effect is far removed from modern aesthetic experience and enjoyment or diversion (the fruit of our hours of leisure), and cuts against the grain of the merely formal approach to the study of literature that predominates in *our* Academy, where the poet plays a harmless game with words that refer to nothing beyond themselves, except, perhaps, to the critic who plays his own game with the poem.[22]

Poetry is threatening in Plato's view for a number of reasons scattered throughout the dialogues, but chiefly because it embodies or at least aspires after a vision of the whole, and concerns what matters most to human beings—virtue and vice, the good life, the gods, what's of value— against a common modern assumption that poets merely express their own personal experience of life; because it celebrates feeble copies of real things (*phantasmata*),[23] and attaches us to particulars, over which we have little control, inviting us to take seriously things we are destined to lose and encouraging us to believe that the loss is somehow tragic. Poetry is threatening because it inflames the passions,[24] and shapes human character more powerfully than almost anything else we know, and in *this* respect resembles what we associate with religion; and because we can be seduced by it even when think we're merely taking harmless pleasure in it. Poetry threatens because, borrowing from Shelley, who almost certainly had Plato in mind, the unchecked poet in an improperly guided polis is the educator and legislator of the human race:[25] before we've reached the age of reason, we already find trivial or degrading things worthwhile, and the poets and artists and mythmakers are largely to blame. We have it on the authority of Herodotus that the Greeks knew little about the gods, before being taught what to believe about the divine by Homer and Hesiod.[26] And we know from Socrates's arguments in the second and third books of the *Republic* what Plato's main character thinks about the influence of his chief rivals upon the development of human character.

If we fail to comprehend or to sympathize with Plato's criticism of Homer, Hesiod, ancient lyric poetry, and the ancient tragedians, it may be because poetry has lost some of its seriousness, except, of course, for those who make it . . . and complain of being poorly valued and misunderstood. The seriousness of poetic and artistic endeavor, still present in Hegel's *Lectures on Aesthetics*, has been replaced by what Robert Pippin calls "the assumption of pluralism" or the view that poets live one sort of life among many possible ways of living.[27] What Murdoch calls "our reverential conception of 'fine art'" is not to be gainsaid, but one still might wonder whether our aesthetic categories of appreciation do justice to what the ancients experienced facing the work of art, where (for us) issues of form and metaphor, characterization, complexity of narrative structure, and originality, tend to dominate the conversation, with playful indifference to content and a failure to register the moral and political reaches of the poet's art. As Christopher Janaway observes in an important study of Plato's criticism of the arts, which means to defend some of what the author of the dialogues has to say about the potential dangers of art, Plato "reveals in us an adherence to aestheticism, the view that some form of pure pleasure or beauty which can be isolated from other states and values is the dominant or sole scale of evaluation for the arts."[28] Along with the paintings of Van Gogh and the poetry of Hölderlin, we also revere, as Heidegger caustically suggests, the "art" of the pastry chef.[29]

From the point of view of Plato's Socrates in the *Republic*, we should wonder about, say, the wisdom of introducing high school students to the depiction of Humbert Humbert's fatal infatuation with Lolita in the novel that bears H. H.'s muse's name. The novel's aesthetic merits are, from the Platonic philosopher's standpoint, beside the point; or to the point, precisely because they threaten to overshadow other dimensions of the work the formalist critic fails in his maturity to appreciate, and that might influence the reader, especially the young reader, more than she and her mentors are prepared to acknowledge.[30]

And yet, if we wish to understand why we find it hard to understand the philosopher's or the moralist's gravity, we should look to Plato's own work; for in a sense our failure to understand the Platonic position signals the philosopher's triumph over stances that now strike many of us as strange, or (more modestly) is the consequence of the rise and spread of an epistemic attitude he was among the first and remains among the best to defend.[31] For it strikes me that many of us share with Plato a set of interrelated assumptions about the nature of poetry and truth, assumptions Plato (or Socrates in the Platonic dialogues) explored and defended at great length, while we tend to take them more or less for granted, that include the following: a collection of poems, however well-integrated and organized about a common theme, never amounts to a philosophical (or scientific) statement of truth (philosophy, or science, unifies its material differently, more rationally, we're inclined to say); poets traffic in mere sentiment, philosophers and scientists in the space of reasons (concepts, propositions, overarching theories, and the like); poets tell us what moves, philosophers and moralists what *ought* to inspire; poetry is personal, despite its claim to reveal the truth about the whole, and truth universal;[32] poets have untested things to say about the nature of the world, while science discloses the structure of reality more reliably, accurately, and methodically. In short, we no longer discover in the poem anything like the *truth* Plato's contemporaries sought in Homer, Hesiod, and the like.[33] And while our current stances may not be informed, at least not directly, by the *Ion* or the *Republic*, it is Plato (or Socrates) who began to codify what counts as knowledge (*epistêmê*) in a way that disqualifies in advance the poem's claim to truth (*alêtheia*).[34] In this respect at least, the author of the dialogues is our contemporary.[35]

But there is, I suspect, another reason why we find Plato's assault on poetry puzzling, and it has more to do with what, after the Cartesian Clauberg,[36] we can call an ontological difference between Plato and his earliest descendants, and certain modern thinkers whose vision of the world we've largely inherited, deepened, and qualified. The quarrel between poetry and philosophy was staged as a *gigantomachia* (a battle of giants, or a titanic contest) over the meaning of being and the good, on the shared assumption that nature is the place of what we call, blandly enough, "values."[37] Poetry was weighed and measured and found philosophically wanting *not* because it wove values and other ostensibly subjective entities into the fabric of the universe, and so failed in our sense to be objective, but because it ascribed worth to the wrong things, and failed to ground and validate a proper sense of the nobility of certain ways of life and the goods they promise in a comprehensive account of the nature of the human soul and the cosmos within which the human being, or the soul embodied, finds itself placed. The criticisms and revisions of poetry in the Platonic dialogues are invariably ethical affairs, which is to say: the world of Plato and the poets the character of Socrates in the dialogues often opposes is above all a world of things that *matter*.[38]

Plato's Philosophic Art and a "Music-Making Socrates"

But surely something is amiss, or at least one-sided, in this brief reca-
pitulation of the quarrel between philosophy and poetry in the Platonic
dialogues, taking the *Ion* as our cue and the better-known discussion of
poetry in the *Republic* as the assumed background. For the same author
who casts his hero in the role of poetry's shrewd philosophic adversary
throughout the dialogues—Plato discusses, and usually criticizes, poetry,
at least indirectly, in at least twelve of the extant works—was also the
paradigmatic philosopher-poet in the minds of Romantic thinkers in
Germany and England (Schelling and Schleiermacher, the brothers Schlegel, and Shelley, translator of both the *Ion* and the *Symposium*, come
readily to mind).[39] Plato's influence reaches into the earlier theological
doctrines of the Cambridge Platonists, as well as the aesthetic and ethical
vision of the Earl of Shaftesbury.[40] And it is instructive to recall, and to
keep steadily in mind, that the conflict between philosophy and poetry
in the tenth book of the *Republic* is a quarrel or feud (*diaphora*), which,
in the context of the dialogue itself, suggests a dispute over shared territory, or a difference between parties who border upon one another's
territory. *Diaphora* is not a mere difference between indifferent things (as
dictionary definitions might lead one to think), but a difference between
rivals and companions of a sort—the sort of difference that might surface between two referees at a sporting event, or, to take a more humble
example from my own field, between rival scholars at a conference. The
reference to the quarrel's antiquity (*palaia*) almost certainly calls to mind
the attacks of earlier philosophers *in verse* upon their poetic rivals.

We should, at the very least, be careful not to saddle the author of
the dialogues with the hostility to poetry one of his dramatis personae
develops in the course of several dialogues, even if the attack is carried
out over several texts and seems, therefore, to give voice to Plato's own
anxieties.[41] In the words of Myles Burnyeat, "Plato is famous for having
banished poetry and poets from the ideal city of the *Republic*. But he did
no such thing. On the contrary, poetry—the right sort of poetry—will be
a pervasive presence in the society he describes." And so to rebut Plato's
critique of poetry, he goes on to suggest, it is not necessary to offer a
defense of poetry as such, but to defend "the freedom of poets to write as,
and what, they wish."[42]

As careful readers of Plato's dialogues are likely to observe, and as
scholars who take the form of the Platonic dialogue seriously are quick
to point out, the philosopher's animadversions to the poetic statement
are difficult to square with certain features of Plato's art and with some

of the views that come forward in his carefully constructed philosophical dramas. The dialogues share with some forms of poetry (I think this is especially true of Rilke's *Elegies*, as I hope to show) an interest in human character (or character types—by which I mean something like basic attitudes toward the world, what it has to offer, and what it means to inhabit the human condition and for what purpose), the values that move particular individuals to express themselves in the way they do, and the oft-conflicting stances toward the most important human issues we discover among those who choose to express and to defend their deepest desires, aspirations, and stances. In sharp contrast to those thinkers who express their positions exclusively in carefully crafted arguments, designed to be as impersonal as possible, Plato's thought combines an interest in argumentative rigor and carefulness with painstaking depictions of the settings and occasions that give rise to philosophical speech, and artful portraits of the sorts of persons who defend certain philosophical views and claims. The only well-known thinker who comes close to Plato for inventiveness of this magnitude is Kierkegaard, whose work has been equally difficult to pin down in more systematic fashion, and whose name is at least as well associated with "irony" as the eccentric figure who appears in most of the Platonic dialogues.

If Socrates's conversation with Ion is meant to be representative, then, or means to make a point about the superiority of philosophic reason to poetic enthusiasm, it is not unimportant that Plato stages the confrontation between the rhapsode and the philosopher in artful, dramatic speech. The lesson is driven home by way of showing, perhaps more convincingly than it would be by merely telling. Socrates's own indictment of poetic enthusiasm at 533e–534b is itself a powerful poetic statement.[43] In the same vein, the philosopher's courage facing death toward the end of the *Phaedo* is at least as eloquent as the earlier arguments for the immortality of the soul worked out in conversation with Socrates's Pythagorean interlocutors, which philosophically minded commentators are swift to criticize on strictly logical grounds. And as astute commentators on the *Republic* cannot help but notice, the attack upon mimetic poetry in the tenth book of the dialogue comes forward in a work that is itself mimetic, a fact that appears to conflict with Socrates's own preference for narrative over mimetic speech-making (or "impersonation") in the third book of the dialogue as well.[44] (Even this needs qualifying; for Socrates makes room in *Kallipolis* for imitation, or impersonation, of good characters, as a preliminary stage in the work, partly a matter of habit, partly a matter of intellect, of *becoming* good; and he appears to allow the imitation of bad types, provided the impersonators are not serious and intend to ridicule what the legislator knows in advance to be unworthy of serious imitation.) Plato himself was certainly aware of the poetic nature of what Socrates was up to in the *Republic*; in the *Laws*, as noted (see note 20 on page 138), he stages a conversation between his legislators and the tragic poets and has the former declare that they, too, are "poets," engaged in the work of making "the most beautiful drama" (the polis), nothing less than an "imitation of the most beautiful and the best of lives."[45] From this perspective, one might almost begin to wonder whether it makes sense to say, as commentators still often do, that Plato was "a great artist as well as a philosopher,"[46] as if the artist is something of an embarrassment, or an inconvenience, for philosophy: the artist and the philosopher in Plato seem to be two sides of the same coin.[47]

It would be no exaggeration or distortion of the work to say that the writings Plato left behind are themselves philosophical poems, provided we interpret "poems" and "poetry" generously enough to make room for those philosophical works that display a dramatic structure, essential to the work's purpose, and that make generous use of poetic motifs (metaphor, allegory, and myth) to advance the work's argument.[48] (Friedrich Schlegel's work of 1795–97, *On the Study of Greek Poetry*, includes a discussion of Plato's "poetical philosophemes or philosophical poems."[49] The quarrel between philosophy and poetry, and the Platonic example of a poetic philosophy, are central to Schleiermacher's editions of Plato's dialogues in German as well [unsurprisingly, as the translation project was conceived, originally, in collaboration with Schlegel], which include substantial interpretations of Plato's thought in his influential "Introduction" to Plato.) And, just as importantly, it is worth reminding ourselves that Socrates himself sometimes speaks in the dialogues as poets and makers of myth are wont to do. If Socrates is often moved to attack poetic modes of discourse in the Platonic corpus, he is also willing to employ some of the tools and techniques of a consummate poet. Sometimes Socrates's use of extant poetic discourse is clearly ironic—I'm thinking of the interpretation of Simonides in the *Protagoras*—but Socrates is often happy, with some important philosophical qualifications, to make use of poetic modes of speech to advance the philosopher's case. And what sometimes, on the surface, appears to be an argument, to be evaluated on logical grounds, turns out to be, by Socrates's own admission, a likely story worth holding for its practical fruits. (I'm thinking here of the conclusion to the argument for recollection and the soul's immortality in the *Meno*, where Socrates tells Meno that the argument may be weak but beneficial in the work of making us "better men, more courageous and less idle.")[50] What are we to make, then, of Plato as philosophical poet and his "music-making Socrates"?[51]

This last point, or question, deserves some fleshing out, before we turn to the topic of poetry's possible claim to truth in the next section, and the world of human meaning opened up in the *Elegies* in what follows upon the heels of the topic of *Dichtung und Wahrheit* (poetry and truth, with a nod to Goethe). That Plato's Socrates inherits certain mythical positions, drawn in some cases, it seems, from Orphic and Pythagorean traditions,[52] and that he makes use of poetic modes of discourse and free mythmaking invention in certain settings within the dialogues, are also commonplaces.[53]

Despite Socrates's claim in the *Republic* that opinions without knowledge (*tas aneu epistêmês doxas*) are ugly (or shameful, *aischrai*),[54] and that philosophy ought to defend itself and its conceptions of things with reasoned argument (what Socrates calls "the longer road" of careful inquiry), the central account of the good, or the idea of the good, in book 6 is more poetic than discursive, trading, as it does, upon certain likenesses between the object of the philosopher's concern and certain aspects of the visible world. (In a revealing aside, Socrates observes that the account of the virtues in book 4 amounts to only "a mere sketch," which calls for completion in "the most finished portrait"; for "any measure of things that falls short in any way of what is, is not a good measure at all, since nothing incomplete is a measure of anything.") In the sequel to the poetic account of the good and the divided line in the opening pages of book 7, Socrates's vision of the human predicament and the effect of *paideia* (education, child-rearing) upon our sense of things comes to voice in the well-known *image* of the cave (this, after Socrates has just demoted images to last place in the order of being at 509e–510a): "Imagine [or picture, visualize, *ide*] human beings living in an underground, cave-like dwelling, with an entrance . . . open to the light and as wide as the cave itself."[55] (Glaucon calls this a "strange image [*Atopon . . . eikona*]" of equally "strange prisoners." Socrates notes, curtly, that they are very much *like us*.)

Turning to other dialogues, we find no shortage of poetic elements and motifs, and frequently at crucial stages of the argument, where modern philosophic readers are likely to expect more careful and rigorous, which is to say less poetic, argument and modes of speech. In the *Sophist*, dialectic is said to be a sort of *purification* of the soul by way of cross-examination.[56] The *Phaedo* models philosophy on the practice of or preparation for death, and several dialogues name the relationship between the forms and the particulars that embody form, much to the sober-minded Aristotle's chagrin, as an instance of "imitation" and "participation." In the *Sophist*, the *interweaving* (*sumplokên*) of forms is said to make speech and statement (*logos*) possible.[57] The *Symposium* makes the worth of the poet's work explicit by assigning poetic labor an important place in the work of begetting in beauty (*tokos en kalô*).[58] And the account of creation in the *Timaeus* is introduced as a "likely account" (*eikôs logos*) and a "likely story" (*eikôs muthos*).[59] Examples could be multiplied indefinitely, but we should also mention here (forgive one more pregnant reference) the wonderful myth of the soul's journey, the conflict between the winged horses attached to the soul's chariot, and the "divine banquet" that forms a central episode in the *Phaedrus*.[60] To say that Plato was ambivalent about poetry (or poetic myth-*making* [the phrase is a tautology]) is a colorless understatement.

The question for philosophy, beyond the philological issues surrounding sources and lines of influence and the multiplication of references, is simply *why*. Or, more precisely: What roles do the poetic elements in Plato's philosophical dramas play? Are they extra-philosophical importations, perhaps meant to persuade a particular interlocutor or set of conversation partners to adopt a stance they would not be able to appreciate from a more philosophical point of view? Are they symbols that can be fully resolved in a discursive account? Or do they suggest a tighter connection between discursive argument and poetic statement than Socrates's official stand on poetry and philosophy in several Platonic dialogues (*Ion, Protagoras, Republic*, for instance, but we could add the *Gorgias* to our list as well)[61] would have us believe?

I suggest that Plato's Socrates has recourse to poetry, or mythmaking, when the problem, or the task, is to capture in speech some sense of the *whole* of things, or to give voice to some aspect of human experience that cannot be readily conveyed in neatly arrayed propositional statements; and when something fundamental or basic—something that, as Aristotle would admit, does not allow for proof but can only be shown—is at issue which grounds our more obviously discursive practices. Some poems read like illustrations of concepts we have ready-made. Others, perhaps the majority of the better kind, deepen our understanding of things we already know, or think we know, something about. But the deeper sort of poetry I take to be at issue, or rather in display, in the Platonic dialogue, often against what the dialogue itself has to say about the poet's worth, gives expression to a vision of a life worth affirming, and a life worth articulating in philosophical thought. Plato's practice, at least, supports the view that poetry or poetic images run throughout both our ordinary and our more sophisticated (philosophical) ways of talking about those things we wish to understand, and in some cases to explain. This doesn't rule out the need for some philosophical, or discursive or scientific, commentary and explanation (Plato's myths and images are rarely allowed to stand on their own); but it does suggest that philosophy begins in discourse that is decidedly *pre-philosophical*, and in a poetic vein that gives philosophy (something) to think.

It is because we *imagine* the soul to be something mortal—perhaps like a wind (*pneuma*) that disperses at death—that we are moved to ask whether something can be said that speaks, discursively, in favor of the soul's immortality; or because we fancy the soul to be something capable of living a life beyond the scope of what we experience here and now that we ask about what its world might be like after death. It is because we *liken* the soul to the city that arguments about justice in the *Republic* are enabled to get off the ground. Our philosophical designs are enabled by the pre-philosophical, and often poetic, ways in which we take an interest in the problems philosophers care about. Poetry provides the tropes, if you will, that nourish the philosophic explication. It is too easy to distinguish between the strictly philosophical and conceptual stretch of a Platonic dialogue and the imaginative and mythmaking component (the image of the divided line, the allegory of the cave, the myth of Er), and to forget that Plato's (or Socrates's) arguments are often built *fundamentally* around pictures or images.

To echo a point I've made elsewhere, the same is very probably true of every philosophical innovator.[62] For Kant, thinking is like *bundling* or *binding things together* (*Verbindung*); in Fichte and Schelling (and possibly for Plato as well [the mind's eye is an important trope for thinking in the Platonic corpus]), thinking is more like seeing (*Anschauung*); in Hegel, it seems to be a matter of returning to yourself and *unfolding* yourself in a shared world of spirit, and sporting with an evolving repertoire of concepts (*Begriffe*, or *graspings*, ways of getting the things of this world *in grip*) in a progressive series of more satisfying *uplifts* (*Aufhebungen*). Even the reductive materialist, working with hard scientific fact, models what we call mind and mental activity on something else which it resembles: the movement of thought is *like* an electrical current traveling along a neuron; memory is *like* the modifications of ribonucleic acid; fear is *like* the agitated outpouring of stress hormones. Or, in keeping with our interest in the tradition inaugurated by Plato, the author of the dialogues often employs metaphors to discuss what his successors come to express in technical terms.[63] So basic is this "metaphorical" way of dealing with fundamental things that we are almost left to wonder whether talk of "metaphor" is even useful any longer. Our thinking about the world works itself out in analogy, is a poetic *reading* of the world, and argument an important afterthought.[64] Plato, I think, understood this, although his commentators have not always followed suit.

But there is another point worth making in this connection, in light of our overarching interest in philosophic and poetic stances on the worth of being human, and finding ourselves cast into a world not of our own making, and over which we often have little control. The Platonic hostility to poetry has often been tied, and for good reasons (think of the way the argument of book 10 of the *Republic* builds upon the epistemological and metaphysical positions developed in books 5, 6, and 7 and the position on philosophy and what comes after death in the *Phaedo*), to wholesale rejection of this world, as unworthy of the philosopher's more serious concerns. In an odd gesture not often noted or developed in the literature on the *Republic*, Socrates supports the philosophical ruler's embodiment of conventional virtues like courage by appealing to the philosopher's indifference to human affairs, which show themselves to be contemptible from the vantage point of "all time and all being." (It's hard to know how to square this with the ruler's need to show some interest in the human affairs of the polis. Socrates develops a similar view of the philosopher's detachment from human affairs in the *Theaetetus*.)[65] But Plato's interest in the poetic regions, sources, and expressions of human consciousness may also evince an attitude of this-worldliness that doesn't sit well with the usual interpretations of Plato's otherworldly leanings, captured in Nietzsche's provocative claim that Christianity is *Platonism for the people*. For the author of the dialogues is keenly aware of the worth of our occasions, the persons we meet, the tropes we inherit, and the models we (sometimes rightly) imitate to dismiss this world as utterly unworthy of our more serious concerns—think of the many depictions of Socrates himself, unshod or bathed, meditating quietly on a porch while the party at Agathon's has already gotten underway, paralyzing Meno like a stingray, unsettling (*atopos*) to Alcibiades, and "like those silenuses that sit in the shops of herm sculptors, the ones that craftsmen make holding reed pipes or flutes; and if they are split in two and opened up, they show that they have images of gods within."[66] It is hard to indict a philosopher with the charge of contempt for this world and its poetry who allows the cicadas to sing, or draws our attention to their singing, if only to remind us of the danger of being immobilized or put to sleep (another metaphor) by song.[67]

Even though Plato's Socrates sometimes works to defend a vision of eternal forms as the grounds of human cognition, he is also eager to seek out evidence in this world for the move beyond it—in opinion's instability, in the conflicting appearances that call for some stable object that allows the appearances to make sense, in the soul's appreciation of the beauty of living form, where, here on earth, we find beauty itself "shining most clearly through the clearest of our senses [sight]," even if our embodied condition is like the soul's imprisonment, "like an oyster in its shell."[68] We need, in short, a this-worldly incentive to hypothesize the existence of the eternal, unchanging beings that enable recognition of what shows, often obscurely, in the visible realm. I say "hypothesize" because I think that the dialogues themselves give no compelling evidence for the existence of the forms that would translate the postulation of form into knowledge of what the *Republic* calls the being of "what is always the same in every respect" and does not wander. The status of the forms, including their existence, is questionable throughout the dialogues, although I'm not sure it makes the best sense to reduce them to articles of faith. Strauss suggestively defines the forms in non-metaphysical terms as the *eternal human problems.*

If there is a world elsewhere, we know nothing about it, as it exists "alone by itself," but can only consider what it *might* be like—that is to say, *imagine* it—with the help of materials furnished by this world of ours. When Socrates begins to fancy life beyond the grave in the *Apology*, for instance, he cannot imagine doing anything but what he's found worth doing in the world he's about to leave behind—settling nothing, but continuing the conversation with worthy companions about the issues he's puzzled over in this Athenian life of his. When he does offer detailed accounts of the soul's journey beyond the visible, myth and image do the bulk of the work.[69] Cribbing from a recent French theorist, who probably had Plato, or Plato's Socrates, in mind: the true life might be absent, but we are in the world.[70]

Chapter 2

✦

Dichtung und Wahrheit Poetry ? Truth

We noted that the Platonist's anxiety facing the poetic statement is rooted in a conception of the world as the place where we discover things to be significant. The poet is found wanting, it was argued, not because he judges the world and our experience of the world to be anchored in "the good" (or the *idea* of the good), or interpretable in ethical categories more broadly construed, but because his way of conveying the significance of human life, ethical, aesthetic, or otherwise, misleads us—attaching us to things of lesser worth, failing to enlighten us about the truth, and inflaming the passions where reason ought to take the lead. Contemporary philosophers might complain that Plato's *Republic* confuses the boundaries between metaphysics (an account of what there is) and ethics or value theory (an account of the good, under some description). But that complaint, justifiable or not, rests upon a clear recognition of Plato's readiness to see the world, or nature, in evaluative terms.

Ours is above all a world of things that matter; and it falls to the poet, the philosopher, and the philosophizing poet to clarify the nature and sources of the significance and value we find in things (pursuits, persons, places, and things more narrowly construed), provided it is true, in Harry Frankfurt's fine phrase, that human beings just *are* "creatures for whom things matter."[1] There can only be a world of things that matter for a creature for whom things matter, and even apathy and despair will prove confirmations of the thesis in the form of unhappy negations and failed or failing affirmations. Indifference, as Heidegger reminds us, is a (deficient) mode of *Sorgen* (caring).[2] Stones and tables cannot be said to be apathetic and cannot be left indifferent, for the simple reason that they cannot be said to care. Whatever else the world may prove to be, then, a cluster of atoms moving and striking each other and sometimes swerving in a void, or the product of a demiurge, informing raw material, or a vast collection of objects to be classified and dissected and movements to be explained, or "a monster of energy, without beginning, without end; a firm iron magnitude of force" endlessly transforming itself,[3] it is first of all (in the order of time and explanation) a context of value and *Bedeutsamkeit* (significance).[4] And where things can be said to be worthwhile, useful, helpful, and significant, their being so is tied to a conception of the good.[5] *This* is the world's primal truth; all other truths about the world, however important and revealing and seemingly comprehensive, are in some sense derivative: where significance and value break off, no world *for us* can be said to be.[6]

All else, or almost everything else, follows from this mattering of, this being affected by, things—joy and despair, pleasure and pain, success and failure, knowledge and ignorance, remembering and forgetting, religion, politics, ethics and art, argument, dialogue, and debate; but also jealousy and envy, cruelty, self-denial, and so on. These are the very tokens of engagement, and signs of significance, and badly defined in the language of doubt and belief, which come later/Deprive the world of things that matter and the world as we know it disappears as well, with nothing left to doubt or to believe, nothing left to decide, no cause for resignation or despair, and no facts to embrace or to reject—taking an interest in the facts begins in romance./

It is about the world in this sense, as the significant context of human concern, that the poet speaks, if Erich Heller is right to say that poetry's meaning is to be sought in "the vindication of the worth and value of the world, of life and of human experience."[7] And if truth is in some sense a relation between utterance and thing (or world), then poetry, too, can be said to be true, as long as the world does not exclude meaning, value, purpose, and the like, and as long as we are not convinced, as Plato's Socrates apparently was, that this world is somehow less real than the eternal forms and patterns that, lying beyond the world, give it shape and significance. All good poetry may be the spontaneous overflow of power-ful feelings, and in *this* sense relative to a subject who *feels*; but "poems to which any value can be attached, were never produced on any variety of subjects but by a man who, being possessed of more than usual organic sensibility, had also thought long and deeply."[8] Our feeling response to form is modified by our thoughts about what exists, and what is "really important to men."[9]

This doesn't have to mean that the poet merely copies a reality fully formed beyond the space of the poem; it could be that the poetic statement helps give body to what there is, or that the poet heightens or intensifies the significance of certain things. Good poets are often cryptic, and often leave the reader with no clear sense of what precisely the poem or some of its imagery is about (Hart Crane comes to mind). But it does entail that the poem, however obscure, is *about* something: "It is concerned with the true stature of things. And being concerned with the true stature of things, all great poetry is realistic."[10] When Rilke lends his voice to house, fountain, gate, pitcher, fruit tree, window, column and tower,[11] when he sings of heroes and lovers scorned and those who died young, he places them all in a valuable world, even when his utterances are laced with melancholy or seem designed to hold despair at bay. That the meaning of a poem is often dark, that we cannot readily say what precisely the poet means, is no counterargument. Poetry should be as dense as the world itself, and as hard to interpret as our most significant experiences. Cribbing from Hilary Putnam: a poem the meaning of which can be put in a nutshell probably deserves to stay there.

All of this may seem too obvious to merit serious discussion. And yet, it may be the very business of philosophy to remark on the ordinary and everyday, the familiar, the near, or what you will, on the assumption that we are ever on the verge of losing sight of what lies closest to us, and fail to understand the soil out of which our explicit conceptions grow.[12] Our theories frequently leave their background conditions out of account, or bring some of the more basic, grounding phenomena into focus poorly. It strikes me that this is especially the case in our ways of talking about the importance of what we care about—meaning, value, significance, and the like—and that this fact helps to explain why many of us no longer find in the poetic statement a truth about the world, but, say, an expression of private experience or a thing of beauty that hangs suspended in a void of mere words, or something that merely amuses and entertains, alongside pastries and other pleasant things.

In "Metaphysics and Ethics" Iris Murdoch argues that the question "What is goodness?" has been replaced by the question "What is the activity of valuing or commending?" "The philosopher is now to speak no longer of the Good, as something real . . . but to analyse the familiar human activity of endowing things with value."[13] We have a handy, ready-made, and familiar vocabulary of more or less interchangeable terms to name what we do when we experience something important or valuable: we endow the world with significance; we project meaning onto the world; we bestow value on what would be worthless without the impact of a valuing mind on indifferent matter. Endowing or projecting or bestowing is the work of a mind straining to find value where there is none, and making up for what the world lacks through its own, perhaps ultimately hollow activity. Our sense of what matters tends almost invariably to express itself in the language of *subjectivism*: something has whatever value it does just because a subject loves it or esteems it or just happens to prefer it.[14] In the absence of a valuing subject there would be only a world of mute and indifferent things. We draw closer to the world, in this view, by bracketing the predicates we ascribe to things when we are most disposed to love them, or to be moved by them in any way.

As Mackie argues, in a provocative account of the invention of right and wrong, values "are not part of the fabric of the world."[15] And if no part of the fabric or furniture of the (objective) world, then certainly values can only be somehow in us: where else are we to discover their sources if we cannot find them out there, in the physical universe? When we cannot discover a value in the realm of neutral fact, it seems natural to look for it in the searching subject. "No doubt if . . . values are not objective they are in some very broad sense subjective."[16]

This view is pervasive enough in the philosophy of value that something must certainly speak in favor of it. Mackie offers several now familiar sorts of arguments to defend the merely subjective nature of our value judgments: arguments from the relativity of what matters across cultures, within a culture over time, and within a culture at any given time; arguments from the strangeness or what he calls the "queerness" of objective values (the fact that we don't encounter values in the same way that we experience stones, plants, animals, and so on); and several arguments targeting specific claims made by objectivists. The arguments from the relativity of what we consider important and worth becoming or doing are perhaps the weightiest. For it does seem obvious that *if* we cannot agree about the value of, say, a landscape, then its beauty just cannot be a property of it but must somehow reside in the eye of the beholder.[17]

Once you've reduced the world as the place where things happen to matter to a residual domain of fact, it comes as no surprise that it doesn't contain anything of moral or aesthetic, social or political value. But why should the world be so thin? Mackie suggests that subjectivism becomes compelling, perhaps unavoidable, once we renounce "a fictitious external authority" that imposes its values upon us.[18] But we might wonder whether Mackie's world is not itself equally fictitious.[19] If we grant, with Frankfurt and Heidegger, that we are fundamentally creatures for whom things matter, then we need a view of the world that makes room for what matters. And while we should make room as well for controversy, dialogue, and debate about what is important and what we ought to do, we cannot begin the work of criticism and revision unless we begin with a realm of fact always already permeated by value. The first task, then, is to get back into a world in which things are allowed to be significant, which is to say: to return to the very world we never left, except in thought.

There may very well turn out to be circumstances within our world in which it makes good sense to ask about an object or a fact, regardless of the value it may or may not possess: that a stone weighs six pounds, that

Rilke was born in Prague on December 4, 1875, that Winston betrays Julia in Orwell's *1984*, and so on *are*, in some sense, matters of fact (or facts about a fiction) with a legitimate claim to objectivity. But what about claims like the following: the world is the objective totality of facts, or justice is the rule of those who just happen to be in power? Is it a mere fact about our lives that our values are not objective? Why so much controversy, then? Why is it unlikely that we will clear up the confusion or put the debate to rest in the same way that we establish the area of a plot of land? There is hardly an issue of deep philosophical or human *Nice* importance that resolves itself into a series of questions to which facts will furnish the answers.

There is, of course, a sense in which Mackie's critique of objectivism is on the right track: if we eliminate ourselves from our picture of the world, if we strip the world of the human element (whatever this turns out to be), and imagine a world of mere things, we (mere observers) discover nothing like values, ethical concerns, and moral requirements. Mattering and worth are not properties that cling to or define purely physical things, like hardness or color. And if our standard of objectivity is an even more elusive view of what there is *an sich*, we are likely to be as disappointed in the philosophical analysis of value as the disaffected lover of traditional metaphysics, convinced by the arguments of Kant's first *Critique*.[20] But once we renounce the fictitious ideal of objectivity, absolute certainty, and the like, we need no longer search for significance inside an equally fictitious mind: meaning and value are in the world, and what we (and poets) say about it, or nowhere.

Chapter 3

The Philosophical World of the *Duino Elegies*

Caveat

As we approach the *Duino Elegies*, it is helpful to remember that there is no discursive substitute for the poem. If poetry could be fully translated into prose, the poet would be a superfluous thing, or, if not altogether unnecessary, a thing of passing significance; and the poem could be sent out into the world, only to dissolve in the prosaic restatement of what it finally means. It would fall to the scientist, or the philosopher, or the moralist, or the aesthetician, to give us the final reckoning, and to complete the work the poet dimly began, without understanding fully what others better placed could puzzle out in a nonpoetic idiom.

We should recall too, and continuing the thread, that those poems that continue to matter mean in abundance, beyond what those who risk interpreting have to say, as weighty expressions of what we might call, after Jean-Luc Marion, the realm of *saturated phenomena*, in opposition to the lean world of things we readily classify and explain or comprehend. *King Lear* hasn't been tapped dry; Wordsworth's *Prelude* arouses controversy still; Wallace Stevens outlives his earliest critics; and we're still translating and talking about Rilke's *Duino Elegies*. Sophocles still gives us to think, and not merely because we take an abstract interest in antiquated ways of thinking about the human condition and its difficulties, and despite the fact that we no longer believe in the gods of Greek tragedy and no longer seek answers at Delphi. Something comes to language in *Oedipus* and *Antigone* that answers a few of the more important questions we put to ourselves, about character, freedom, and fate, illusion and the price of disillusionment, the conflict between the public and the private spheres, and the invisible limits within which our lives, often unhappily, unfold, despite what we think we know and how firmly we believe ourselves to be in control. It is, perhaps, a mark of the best poems that the more they've been interpreted, the more we feel moved to reinterpret: the commentaries solicit more . . . commentary. The meaning of a true poem, we've

The power of poetry

grown accustomed to say, is *inexhaustible*, or (more modestly) resists our efforts to restate it *so far*.

A great poem adapts itself to unexpected horizons and undergoes, in Malraux's helpful way of thinking, as many metamorphoses as we, collectively and individually, undergo.[1] Its meaning changes with our own shifting circumstances, like a thing that refuses to be buried with its maker. And the best interpreters escape oblivion, when they do, because their readings contain something of the density and obscurity of their originals, because a good critic is also a decent poet. The world of the *Elegies*, cribbing from Thoreau, is larger than our conceptions of it.

But we don't know what we think, and so have no definite conceptions, until we venture to speak: the poem lives partly in the conversations and monologues it provokes, partly in the poems written under its influence. Our silences can be pregnant, and wise. Sometimes they bear witness to our poverty. Truly solitary appreciation, unshared, is a useless thing and probably narcissistic. The real danger is to believe that we've finished what we've only just begun, or to think that we can do for others what we've done for ourselves. In the best and weightiest of things, all help is probably indirect, as Emerson and Thoreau never tire of reminding us.[2]

Introducing the World of the *Elegies*

The world, we have argued, and cribbing from Heidegger, is a space of significance and meaning. But what it means and how, and why we should be moved to love the world, assuming we should, are nothing obvious. To give our assent to this proposition is merely the beginning of our human work. Our thesis is an *archê*, a first principle in Aristotle's sense, is something from which other things can be said to flow: what remains is to puzzle it out, and the measure of our labors is an entire life. Why should it be easy to measure and speak accurately, where this must sometimes mean *poetically*, of the weight of things? It is easy, perhaps, to play at pushpin, or to bake a loaf of bread, or to enjoy the coming of dawn, fresh from a sound night's sleep. But to give our fullest possible assent to *this* world is, perhaps, the most difficult thing of all. So many things seem to conspire against our affirmations. And our innocence is among the first things to depart. The world is meaningful, but the meaning and the worth of things are fragile, and a puzzle from first to last.

The world of the *Elegies*, in keeping with their genre, is one of failure and loss, a world of *Leiden* and *Klage* (suffering and lament), centered on a meditative poet, struggling to come to grips with the significance of mortal things, and probing various strategies of assenting to a world that takes away as much as it gives.³ The seriousness and dignity of the poet's final affirmation and *Rühmen* (praise) are, as we shall see, made possible by the hard reality these poems refuse to shirk, and a compelling sense that happiness, commonly understood, is not our lot: the constancy contained in the idea of being happy doesn't fit the life of a mutable being in a fickle world.⁴ If the *Elegies* offer consolation at the end of "a purely affirmative day,"⁵ also in keeping with their genre, it is the hard-won fruit of our most difficult endeavors. It is the consolation that comes of *integration*—death in life, pain in joy, sorrow in affirmation, and transience in what endures, or duration in what flees—and fashions for itself "pearls of grief."⁶

The high argument of the *Elegies* offers a poetic solution to what we could call in a philosophical key the problem of skepticism, where this is shorthand for the difficulty of finding good reason to give our assent to something of no small importance (the reality of the external world or the existence of other minds comes readily to mind), against initially compelling reason to suspend belief or trust. If the *Elegies* place themselves in a setting of doubt, and help to ground our uncertainty or merely to give it voice, and so echo one of the principal anxieties of modern philosophy (that the world may be somehow and permanently out of reach), the skeptical malady they evoke is hardly an academic affair. They do not ask whether the world can be said to exist (a problem which probably troubles nobody's sleep), but whether the world is worth loving and our existence in it worth affirming; not whether we have good enough reason to believe in the reality of other minds, but how we can sustain our affection when the beloved betrays us, or our children die before they've had a chance to live, and thoughts of our own mortality unsettle our commitments. Cartesian arguments for the reality of *res extensa* (the [spatially] extended thing), grounded in the benevolence of a god above deceiving, or Kantian refutations of subjective idealism, anchored in the impossibility of gaining access to a mental state without reference to something external to the mind, overcome, at best, a slender *metaphysical* doubt we shelve when hungry or in pain. Even if the arguments prove valid, they do little more than vindicate a belief (we never fully renounced) in a world (we never left) we find *different* sorts of reasons, and weightier, to doubt, and to doubt in another key. The skepticism of the *Elegies* is above all an *erotic* affair.⁷

We should expect the sources of disbelief or slackened conviction that trouble the elegiac poet to be somewhat more robust, then, and more genuinely threatening than the reasons tiresomely enumerated by philosophers and skeptics to doubt the veracity of the senses, or to wonder whether reason alone is able to teach us substantial truths about the existence of the soul, god, and the like. They are, more fittingly, reasons implicated in our loving attachment to the things of this world. They provoke no *mere* doubt, when they assail, but something far more like melancholy or despair, where epistemological worries give way to something along the lines of pessimism, and what Nietzsche called *nihilism*—the sense that our values and efforts to realize them come in the end to nothing, or are sustained in illusion, or can only be possible in a state or stage of innocence we are fated eventually to lose. If we are the sorts of creatures who can lose our grip on the world, it isn't because we seem to find occasional reasons to doubt whether or not this tree here exists, but because we believe we've discovered reasons to doubt whether it matters that the world *is* at all, despite the fact that it obstinately persists: that the world can still *be* when it no longer fully *means* is a more terrifying prospect than the same stick appearing sometimes crooked, sometimes straight.

Some of the more powerful lines in the *Elegies* give voice to a terrible sense of the transience of important things. Whatever the world turns out to be, it is the place where the things that matter, and matter most, depart. In the "Second Elegy," the poet laments the coming and going of our strongest emotions, in contrast with the enduring self-presence of the Angel, whose outpouring is always an ingathering, and who experiences, paradoxically enough, only untroubled "tempests of feeling": "But we, when we feel, evaporate; alas, we breathe / ourselves out and away; from ember to ember our fragrance grows fainter."[8] In a line that evokes Schiller's famous complaint, we are reminded that the appearance of beauty in the human face, a source of so much agitation and ecstasy in youth, always "moves on." And this is quickly generalized to include everything that apparently moves and, by moving deeply, defines us: "Like dew from the morning grass, / what is ours rises from us, like the heat from a hot dish / of food." At first, this fugitive quality of our experience is set in contrast to the solid and stable world of things, like trees, and the houses in which we dwell, or the Attic steles in which the ancients found repose. But in the affirmative "Seventh Elegy," the poet reminds us that houses and temples and other more durable things are as fleeting as we are. Already in the "First Elegy" we hear, in connection with deserted lovers: Remaining is Nowhere. And the burden of what remains of the *Elegies* is to explore possible ways of coming to terms with this primal fact about the world in which we find ourselves uneasily thrown.

The elegy has been defined, usefully enough if roughly, as "a lyric . . . suggested by the death of an actual person or by the poet's contemplation of the tragic aspects of life. In either case, the emotion originally expressed as a lament finds consolation in the contemplation of some permanent principle."[9] But this is likely to mislead the reader of the *Duino Elegies*, especially if "some permanent principle" calls to mind the likes of a self-revealing god and his undying reassuring love for his creatures, an eternal realm of intelligible being, a lasting social order, embodying justice, or an enduring ethical law that clarifies choice. Even the angels, sources of endless controversy in the interpretation of these poems, appear to signify an order of existence out of reach for the lamenting poet, or accessible (as the "First Elegy" suggests) at the cost of annihilation, and repudiated, it seems, as authentic comforting sources, assuming comfort should be our aspiration. There is something inhuman about the angelic way of being, and its beauty is terrifying because we cannot find our*selves* (preserved) in it.

If our sufferings, the very source of the poet's suspended outcry in the "First Elegy," find no home *there*, among the angels, it is surely because we cannot imagine a life there, in those outlandish regions where fullness reigns and nothing seems to happen. We'd lose in the angelic ethereal— love, or any human passion which attaches us to mortal things, lives in uncertainty and reversal, and brings us often enough to grief, and that striving to overcome obstacles, physical, psychological, and social, that makes as much of life as anything we know, but also religion and political engagement and struggle which, if Tocqueville is right, promise release from a narrowing self-preoccupation and attachment to merely material well-being,[10] and that exquisite sense of being placed among things the beauty of which seems tied to their fragility, as Wallace Stevens reminds us in "Sunday Morning." ("Death is the mother of beauty; hence from her, / Alone, shall come fulfilment to our dreams / And our desires.")[11] And it is, of course, impossible to imagine Rilke's angels making art. What could they seek to memorialize in their endless self-mirroring, almost smug, if they were capable of that all-too-human vice? If the poet is able to bring the angels into his orbit, it can only be because he possesses something they lack, if only the possibility of lacking and the fructifying sting of an absence that, unsettling and sometimes, like one's own death, merely imagined or anticipated or, like the past, still somehow present, gives birth to speech. As Rilke writes in 1922—the very year the poet completed the *Elegies* and composed the *Sonnets to Orpheus*—in the voice of a Young Workman, "Here is the angel, who doesn't exist, and the devil, who doesn't exist; and man, who does exist, stands between them; and, I can't help it, their unreality makes him all the more real to me."[12]

The angels seem to represent the permanent human tendency, or temptation, to seek refuge in the permanent and its empty silence.[13] The *Elegies*, I suggest, lament the loss of what the traditional elegy sought out and embraced: the days of Tobias are no longer our own.[14] The angels of the *Elegies* are, paradoxically, messengers without a message, speechless; or, in a curious reversal of the traditional figure, they are called upon to hear the poet's song of praise and to be astonished by what we can accomplish in *this* world.[15] The "Tenth Elegy," looking further ahead, brings the cycle to a close with a story of Lament, as though that were our proper strain, and the world that makes us shudder and grieve our proper if fleeting home, a world in which sometimes, unexpectedly, or against our gloomiest expectations and upsetting our sense of happiness rising, "a happy thing falls."[16]

In between the opening refusal of surrender to the angelic order and the wisdom of the closing lines, more evocative and oracular than definitive, the *Elegies* explore a series of attempts, in life and in art, to work out a satisfying solution to the everlasting problem of being human:[17] to be in the midst of what departs and to be departing, to find reasons to doubt an almost natural longing for the eternal, to be enamored with what everyday life seems to conspire against, and to hope against probability for a more meaningful life, embracing a death, of one's own.[18]

Art in the City of Grief

A philosopher not unrelated to our poet has claimed that optimism is a wicked way of thinking.[19] It is at least superficial, or presumptuous, even when backed by eloquence. As Kant reminds us, even the more refined optimism of Leibniz presupposes that we can fathom the mind of god, or survey the infinite extent of possible worlds, in order to pronounce this world of ours the best. Optimism is a comparative way of thinking, as all thinking probably is, that presumes and promises more than it can possibly deliver. We cannot overleap ourselves, and the best of all possible worlds remains a fiction as long as we live and think in time and as occasion merits. If it encourages indifference toward the more terrifying prospects of a life lived forward and in uncertainty, and hardens the philosopher against the plight of the struggling unfortunate, optimisms may well be immoral as well as shallow.

There's nothing shallow or precious or optimistic in Rilke's mature poetry. The triumphant note that sounds in the poet's most moving verse has its melancholy *basso continuo*. The famous panther of the *New*

Poems is, after all, wearily confined behind a thousand bars, *und hinter tausend Stäben keine Welt* (and behind the thousand bars no world). And so, perhaps, are we, at least some of the time. And the site of the poet's most despairing thoughts in the *Duino Elegies*, bordering pessimism, is the city—call it Paris, the place of Malte's anxieties, the squares of the milliner Madame Lamort in the well-known "Fifth Elegy," and the unnamed symbolic city of grief in the "Tenth Elegy."

The city and its life are easy enough to slander. De Quincey, Kantian enthusiast and melancholy English opium-eater, was haunted in London by "gloom and uncertainty" and a "sense of desertion and utter loneliness." London is the place of the exile, the world of "the houseless vagrant of every clime."[20] The sprawling urban metropolis is a labyrinth without a center, and (as in Baudelaire, subsequently interpreted with the help of Benjamin) the place where human eyes "have lost their ability to see" and glance meets glance in vacancy.[21] The preternaturally vital and cheerful Dickens describes London in November as so much "mud in the streets," the air permeated by smoke, the pedestrians "jostling . . . in a general infection of ill-temper," and defiled by "fog everywhere."[22] Even Emerson, celebrant of almost everything as evidence of a universe that remains always to the core unhurt by what stings each of its disaffected and disappointed offspring, found in the great cities too little room for the human senses.[23] The city, in short, has come to symbolize the loss of all we associate with Paradise: closeness to nature and the divine, community, stability, order, physical health, and spiritual sanity.

The world of the city looms large in Rilke's life and work. And much of what the poet has to say merely repeats what's become a commonplace complaint. Echoing the despairing tones of a large and lengthening literary tradition, *The Notebooks of Malte Laurids Brigge* lends voice to the misery and abandonment of life in Paris,[24] where people only seem to come to live, but in truth to die, and where death itself—a constant theme of Rilke's poetry—has become something "ready-made, you just have to slip on. You leave when you want to, or when you're forced; always no effort: Voilá votre mort, monsieur."[25] Where old haggard women display pencils and other unimportant things with infinite care and knowing glances, men battle with their own collars for reasons that remain obscure, and at carnival time the faces of the people ooze with laughter "like pus from an open wound";[26] where faces themselves are insensibly worn away over the years and only a "bare flayed head without a face"[27] remains; where memory decays, and the odor of urine, soot, and rancid grease assaults the poet's senses near a dilapidated wall; and everything possesses "a stubborn permanence, all this endures in itself and, jealous of everything that is, clings to its own dreadful reality."[28] In this climate and setting, it seems, it is enough to survive: "The main thing was, being alive. That was the main thing."[29] Writing to Lou Andreas-Salomé on July 18, 1903, the poet complains: "Paris was for me an experience like military school.[30] Then I was seized with fear, just as now I am gripped by terror at everything that in unspeakable confusion is called life."[31] Paris, at the very least, stands for a part, and an ever-expanding part, of the world the poet must discover some reason to affirm, despite the overwhelming reason to reject, or at least to stand scornfully aloof.

But Paris is also the place where the poet met Rodin, through Clara, sculptor at Worpswede, student of the famous artist, and eventually Rilke's wife, and mother of his daughter, Ruth. Rodin stood always in Rilke's mind for the triumph of art over everything that, small and large, conspires against it, where the "ancient enmity between life and the great work" is no longer felt, and everything petty and degrading is blissfully relegated to a house that means nothing, "perhaps a shelter from the rain, a roof overhead for periods of sleep; it concerned him not the least and it placed no burden on his loneliness and composure."[32] In Rodin Rilke saw the embodiment of the motto (the sculptor's favorite): *Qu'il faut travailler, travailler toujours* (It is necessary to work, always to work).

Paris is where the poet's persona in *Malte* learns to see and, we might add, to sympathize with the lowly, the poor, the downtrodden and outcast. Paris is the place where the sentimentalist comes to grief against the empty reality of the dissatisfied, and those unfortunates dwell, who should feel more unhappiness with what the world has managed to give than they apparently do. And Paris is the place where Rilke created some of his finest early verse, the so-called *Ding-Gedichte* (thing-poems).[33]

The city: a place of misery and a place of art, of despair and of ecstasy. It is at least, as it was for Socrates, a school for understanding the human condition; for trees and lakes, however lovely, don't tell us what to think, and poets, however scornful, live among men, and argue against their more contracting infatuations, often in sympathy, knowing about them and sensitive to what circumstance can make of an innocent life. If Rilke's attitude toward the city was ambivalent, his was a fruitful ambivalence.[34]

The city: temporary home of the acrobats. The "Fifth Elegy," written last and within a few days of the affirmative, almost mythmaking "Tenth Elegy," is perhaps the most despairing and realistic in the cycle; dedicated to Frau Hertha von Koenig, once owner of Picasso's *Les Saltimbanques* (now housed in the National Gallery in Washington), and of a house in Munich where the poet lived for several months in 1915, it can be read as a meditation on the bleak inner reality of the acrobatic *Fahrende* (wayfarers, vagrants), depicted by the painter in a rare moment of stillness and lacking expression, and as an account of the fate of art in the specious squares of that "endless showplace" Paris, where Madame Lamort (mistress of death) creates out of ribbons, rosettes, and artificial fruits "the cheap winter hats of fate." Here, in the cityscape of art and artifice, the poet seems to be suggesting, it becomes difficult to distinguish between what *is* and what merely *seems* to be, and everything runs the risk of degenerating into senseless automatism, at the expense of those vast trembling inner spaces, the veritable sites of meaning the poet will come to celebrate in the "Seventh" and "Ninth" elegies as soil and home of the poet's affirmations.

As the "Fifth Elegy" opens, we find the acrobats falling through "oiled and slippery air back / to the threadbare carpet . . . abandoned and alone in the world." They resemble the puppet of the "Fourth Elegy" (praised, provisionally, for being full and without pretense), but these are *human* puppets, endowed with just enough consciousness of life to be dissatisfied, and to feel pent up in a world brought into being and spurious life "by an ever discontented will." And the tattered carpet that cushions their landing is, in one of the poet's more striking images, "stretched out like a bandage, as if the suburban / sky had battered the earth there."[35]

It is a disconcerting picture. We tend to think of acrobatics as *graceful* movement, and are astonished facing the complicated bodily tricks and feats of strength the performers sometimes show, as though the body, otherwise dark, resistant, and clumsy, had finally yielded to intelligence and the thinking demand for moving form. For those of us tempted to romanticize the circus life, as Dickens came close to doing in *Hard Times*, Rilke reminds us that life among this group of wayfarers is hard, and less meaningful than we, in our reveries and sentimental abandonments, like to think; and they are not, after all, as free as we enjoy imagining, but controlled by a will apparently not their own, just as the male lover in the "Third Elegy" is driven by the chthonic forces of sexuality, save that here, in the barren world of the "Fifth," there is no joyful surrendering to the "wilderness" within, but only a dull uncomplaining confinement within the walls of human artifice. And their artificial movements, all too easy now in a world built up in the quick formation of habit, of need and untutored desire, merely mimic the tree's more patient growth, hastening through the seasons—"rushing like water in a few minutes through spring and summer and autumn"—and bearing only unripe fruit that falls hard upon a grave.

And those of us who watch, who gather in the city in order to be entertained? The spectator is no visionary, although the poet gives the gawker's experience pregnant voice, and tries at first "around this / center" the image of "the rose of watching" blooming and shedding its leaves. This at first evokes in the knowing reader Rilke's long-standing fascination with the rose, and calls to mind the inscription the poet wrote for his own gravestone: *Rose, oh reiner Widerspruch, Lust, / niemandes Schlaf zu sein unter soviel/ Lidern* (Rose, oh pure contradiction, joy, / to be nobody's sleep under so many/ lids). But the center, the acrobatic spectacle we are privileged shortly to behold, becomes a pestle/pistil (*Stempel*), we aren't sure which (the German allows Rilke to equivocate, fruitfully), "surrounded by the pollen / of its own dust" and giving birth in escalating artifice to a "false fruit" without awareness and "an easy specious smiling discontent." It is a parody of the organic (or an account of the organic transforming itself into the inorganic, the latter uncertainly asserting itself at first and finally taking over), and a reminder that life is lived elsewhere, that our carnival smiles cover our unhappiness. We watch in order to forget, and conceal our dissatisfaction beneath a paining, unconvincing smile. For a moment we *feel* more alive, but the desert stands still beneath the flurry of activity that mimics fumblingly the slow growth of a living thing, making dead leaves, dust, and false fruit masking *inquietude*.

Only the fleeting loving look of the boy toward his "seldom tender mother" redeems the scene; and even this "rarely tried expression" is quickly lost in the young acrobat's body, as the hand of the man clapping calls for the leaping and the pain in the soles of the feet chases away, with all the force of a dying hungry animal, the tears in his "still living eyes."

"And yet, blindly, / the smile . . . . ." It remains for the poet, summoning the angel, to remember and preserve in an apothecary's urn with "flowery swirling inscription" what fleeting trace of human feeling remains in a life refusing life: *Subrisio Saltat*. The fleeting smile of the unfortunate acrobat, like the Lament for Linos in the "First Elegy," is an artist's promise, and a token of redemption to come.

Nature, Wilderness, the Lives of Animals

The *Elegies* often gesture beyond the iron cage of human design, and the empty, uninspiring artifice of metropolitan life, where we are not at one, having "lost connection . . . with the earth,"[36] toward a way of life more fruitfully in tune with the order of nature, and toward Nature itself—dark, mysterious, but sure of itself, and source of poetic utterance, "great, indifferent, mighty Nature."[37] And all the greater, perhaps, and inspiring for not needing us, like the "early departed" of the "First Elegy."

Like so many themes explored in Rilke's mature poetry, this one can be traced back to the poet's earliest musings. Writing of the colony of painters living and working in Worpswede two decades earlier, with two influential trips to Russia behind him and fruitful Paris days still ahead, Rilke laments the loss of contact with nature in the great cities, where people "hang, as it were, in the air, hover in all directions, and find no place where they can settle."[38] And this, the poet suggests, stands in sharp contrast to the life of Millet's shepherds and peasants, "who pass their lives nearer to Nature," although nature is no less hard on them than it is on the painter and his civilized admirers. Children, too, do not (yet) see in nature "something to be exploited as much as possible," but live like-mindedly "within her, like the smaller animals, entirely at one with the happenings of forest and sky and in innocent, obvious harmony with them."[39]

If the *Elegies* explore the burden of human consciousness, and examine a few of the more compelling strategies for coming to terms, affirmatively, with the human condition, it is hardly surprising that unconscious Nature's appeals should enter into the poet's language and vision; for we've come almost naturally to expect (after the romantic movement, in the wake of Thoreau and Emerson, John Muir and the Sierra Club, and in an era of national parks and international campaigns to preserve wilderness) pristine nature, or at least a part of nature no longer destined for human consumption and use, to serve as a healthy antidote to civilization and its discontents: "in Wildness is the preservation of the World."[40] We should, however, be cautious not to identify one of several strategies explored by the narrator of the *Elegies* with the final stance achieved, or suggested, by the end of the cycle; this stance, too, may prove to be something like what Joshua Landy in an important study of Proust calls the narrator's "provisional conclusions."[41]

As early as the "First Elegy," natural phenomena, including the times and the seasons, are offered as pregnant and promising things to be noticed, because somehow *worthy* of attentive regard, beyond our sterile confinement within the *gedeuteten Welt* (interpreted world), where "discerning animals already note / that we are not truly at home": a tree on a hillside, the spring, stars, dissolving night. When the poet comes to speak, obscurely, of the terrible majesty, the *mysterium tremendum*, of angelic being, the images are drawn partly from the natural world: mountain ranges, ridges red with dawn, pollen of the flowering godhead. And in the final stanza of the "Second Elegy," the poet casts his longing in the language of nature, as a desire for some "pure, contained, slender / strip of our own fruitful land, something human, / between stream and stone."

Nature in these early invocations[42] stands outside the merely human realm, silently and serenely, and invites us to enter its precincts, or at least to contemplate without jealousy and rivalry its beauty and sublimity.

More often, as we move further along in the cycle and disgust with human things sometimes gains the upper hand, the poet contrasts the sure spontaneity of the natural order, especially the movements of animals, with the uncertainty and belatedness of human endeavor, as in the chiding figure of the fig tree in the "Sixth Elegy," or "the birds migrating knowingly" and the lions knowing nothing in their majesty of weakness in the "Fourth Elegy," rebuking those of us who "intending one thing, / already feel the expense of another." Nature, the poet seems to be saying, is all healthy instinct, even when it seems in particular cases to fail; *we*, on the other hand, are all consciousness, conflict, and disease, and failing before we even begin.[43] (Even the puppet of the "Fourth Elegy" fares better than we do: "I will / endure the shell and the wire and the face / formed of surfaces." The puppet, at least, is *full*.)

Rilke's naturalism, if we can call it that, skates along the borders of metaphysics in the "Eighth Elegy," on the *Kreatur* and its relation to what the poet calls "the Open." This short elegy, dedicated to Rilke's friend Rudolf Kassner, is a parable of vision, the poet's proper domain as a seer. And it is, oddly enough, almost more despairing than the vision of acrobatic life in the "Fifth," despite (or perhaps because of) what it praises in the animal's inscrutable gaze, without parallel in our own. Here, in this celebration of the animal's relation to what *we* call the world, it's as if the most important thing to be imagined and desired happened to be locked up eternally behind doors no human effort or ingenuity could possibly open—an almost Calvinistic image of inevitable damnation, except that nobody can be saved. This isn't the first time Rilke had imagined a natural world out of step with the demands of human life: in the essay on Worpswede, spring comes (in adolescence) when we are sad, and roses bloom, and birds sing despite our melancholy; we smile in "the heavy days of November" and "a long sunless winter follows" without our complicity.[44] Sometimes nature accords with us and mirrors our moods; sometimes it doesn't. But what appears earlier to be the unhappy consequence of mere accident, perhaps remediable, takes shape as necessity and destiny in the "Eighth Elegy": our inability is congenital, like original sin.

The elegy voices dissatisfaction with the (human) world of objects that seems our natural lot. Through no apparent fault of our own, we see always only things interacting with other things, in a world of conditioned things, "always world / and never nowhere without the Not," never "that pure / undivided element which one breathes and endlessly *knows* and does not desire." And we are in consequence always dissatisfied: for we are born of the desire for infinity, and we always discover *form*, and limit. We seek the unconditioned and find only (conditioned) things, as the poet Novalis lamented. A painter sets out to capture a landscape, and realizes only scraps and the fruit of half-hearted effort. The novelist is haunted by the idea of the perfect narrative, but he will not and cannot succeed in putting an end to the history of the novel. A lover or a friend sees at first a promise of ocean, and finds, in the end, a stagnant, limited pond. Every moment of fulfillment is an occasion for dissatisfaction, opening onto an uncertain future. Our mind is condemned to encounter serially, and to think discursively, not intuitively, like the god of an earlier metaphysical theology. The mind stands on *this* side, the world on the other; and the latter presents what we fumblingly recombine in a poor image of what we thought we saw. "This is what destiny means: to be opposed / and nothing save this and opposed forever." We arrange the world, and watch it fall apart. We anticipate, and are disappointed, are here for now, building up ephemeral edifices and phantoms of the brain, but "always taking leave" and haunted by death, where the limits we've come to accept, even to love, are overcome against our will. If only we could cast our glance beyond the differentiated spaces of objects and into the open, we'd be free; but this is just what we cannot do—we try, we fail, "and once again there comes to be a world."

The animal (*Kreatur*), by contrast, sees with all its eyes the *open*, a space without form, limitless, "into which flowers open / themselves endlessly." Because the animal knows nothing of the limits within which we confine ourselves, or are confined, it knows nothing of what we call *death*: "the free animal has its perishing always behind itself / and God in front, and when it moves, it moves / in eternity, as wells and fountains move." And so, absorbed in a sort of *nunc stans*, its being is *for it* endless, unfathomable, and pure, and *comprehensive*: "And where we see the future, it sees the All / and itself in the All and healed forever."[45] What for us is a task, assuming we can accomplish it (and the elegy gives reason to doubt that we can), comes to the animal naturally, as its birthright and unchosen way of being. The animal, more than the angel of the "First Elegy," is "creation's spoiled offspring."

It is easy to criticize this apparent affirmation of animal life, set in contrast to the alienation of the human animal from the "Open." If we were the untutored primates of wild nature or taught by nature's lessons only, doubt and disunity would be unthinkable: our savage movements would be spontaneous always, and matters easily settled by the happy force of instinct, and always somehow in the right because not possibly in the

wrong—a desire without a thought is not an object of possible evaluation. We'd be confined in nature's narrow precincts; and mind would not
be crowded by the unsettling thought. We'd be but dimly conscious of our
motions and pleased and pained by their nearest result. Conflict would
not rend the mind's fabric nor paralyze the will. More powerful emerging force would put to rout each doubt (before it *became* a doubt), in an
undying present, unlinked to the settled past and the uncertain future;
and all would be action and reaction, success and failure, without con-
ceivable regret. Being so thoroughly at one, we'd have no need to seek
"escape [from] the sophistication and the second thought."[46]

But we are animals that think and speak. And we reason in community,
in light of tainted thoughts, and moved by dark desire. We gravitate *sometimes* sanely toward the brook and the overhanging leaves, and delight in
forest glen and mountain lake, thinking nothing of possession, taking our
pleasure and joy in what fecund *natura naturans* gives and takes away
in a perpetual movement of color and form. But we just as often cast a
sidelong leering glance at someone we'd like vainly to own, entranced by
mere form and shell, and having in mind besides a pleasing arrangement
of fleshy parts nothing but what we fancy to be the other's depth. It is
possible, of course, to be mistaken, as the animal, in a sense, can never
be; our affections can prove sadly misplaced. We are cozened, perhaps, by
ill-framed thoughts of power and possession and tendered a fool. But this
is because, unlike the animal, we *have* depths to be mistaken about. If we
cannot live up to the animal's relation to the "Open" it is because, precisely and fruitfully because, we are troubled *lovers*, and troubled in ways
that the animal, with all things lying happily behind, and settled before
they even had a chance to begin, can never be. Heidegger's notorious
critique of Rilke's celebration of the "Open" in the "Eighth Elegy," conveniently summarized by Eric Santner in a recent volume on "creaturely
life,"[47] is, I think, misplaced; and unfair precisely for failing to situate the
elegy within the context of the cycle as a whole, which, as I've been trying
to show all along, means to explore competing strategies for coming to
be (uneasily) at home in the interpreted world.[48] But *that* task falls to the
(human) lover, a figure Heidegger passes over in silence.

Lovers Satisfied and Stilled

The *Elegies* are, collectively, a sort of love poem, struggling throughout
to find an appropriate object, against the permanent threat of loss and
the evanescence of all mortal things; and as it turns out, in a gesture that

(perhaps not by accident) resembles a line traced out by Nietzsche, nothing less than the world as a whole will satisfy the poet's insatiable *erôs*, as it comes to voice (and *being*) in the space of the poem.[49] As the young poet, writing of Worpswede, suggests toward the beginning of his life as a poet, "the theme and purpose of all art would seem to lie in the reconciliation of the individual and the All, and the moment of exaltation, the artistically important moment, would seem to be that in which the two scales of the balance counterpoise one another."[50] And toward the end of this early essay: "The artist's function is—to love the enigma. All art is this: love, which has been poured out over enigmas—and all works of art are enigmas surrounded, adorned, and enveloped by love."[51]

If Rilke speaks so often, and often so scornfully, of love in the *Elegies*, it is because love generates the poet's problem (the opening cry of the "First Elegy" strikes *this* ear, at least, as the outcry of a disaffected lover, on the verge of falling out of love with the world, and the final words in the "Tenth," preceded by the affirmative "Seventh" and "Ninth," seem to be those of a reconciled counterpart); and this because the story of human life is always and essentially a love story; for love is the first cause of all we do and undergo, even when we're not thinking about our erotic investments and even, or more obviously, when we are jealous or when we hate, and even when, paradoxically, we no longer feel the force and burden of *erôs*, in apathy or skepticism or despair; because love (or care) is the very ground of our being: "There is no force in the world but love," as the poet writes to Simone Brüstlein in the early months of 1921.

The least erotic man (or woman) is merely a shallow lover, but a lover all the same; our pathologies and healthier conflicts are romantic; and our greatest disappointments are (I'm tempted to say "by definition") failures in the difficult shared and solitary work of love. Our greatest successes are, more obviously perhaps, fruit and evidence of a love that managed somehow, we often cannot say precisely how, to turn out well. When Pascal formalized the three great approaches to life, he singled out the body, the mind, and *above all* love, at once lowest and highest, which is to say the greatest: *ordo amoris* is the order of our very lives, and what from one point of view is origin is from another goal. This is, perhaps, why it is always possible to trace the most sublime aspirations back to the ridiculous, or the immature: in the highest reaches of the human spirit there persists something of the archaic desire. As Nietzsche notes, in what is too easy to see, after Freud, as evidence of a disillusioning physiological frame of mind, one's sexuality extends up to the highest pinnacle of one's spirituality. Beneath our obvious divisions, conflicts, and dislocations, we are one continuous erotic being.

And yet, some of Rilke's most powerful lines in the *Elegies* express grave doubts about loving and being loved.[52] And elsewhere: in the "Requiem für eine Freundin," the poet's meditation on the life and death of the painter Paula Becker, the poet laments in a gesture that borders on solipsism "that someone / took you from your mirror." (The unnamed someone is the artist's husband: "in him I accuse them all: man.") The poem reads more like a requiem for the demise of an artist still living, bent by the marital bond and a narrow conception of what womanhood requires to a life of conformity and artistic sterility, than a lament over the painter's actual death. As Ralph Freedman notes in his biography of the poet, Paula was in Rilke's imagination an artist "who died of being a woman."[53] This pressure to conform, in loving, to sterile conventions and empty forms takes on almost cosmic dimensions in the poem: "For somewhere there is an ancient conflict / between our life and the great work." As it so often happens in Rilke's meditations on love and its fragility, the lamenting voice in the "Requiem" flirts with a solitary's definition of loving: "We have, when we love, this one thing alone: / releasing each other; for holding on / comes easily and we have here nothing to learn"— "loving means being alone." Hard words, and paradoxical; and a poet's creed—but poets sometimes tell difficult truth.

Writing in a more prosaic vein seven years earlier to a young aspiring poet named Kappus, Rilke warns, in a passage worth quoting at length (if only to place the dissatisfactions of the *Elegies* in a clearer light), that

> young people err so often and so grievously in this: that they . . . fling themselves at each other, when love takes possession of them, scatter themselves, just as they are, in all their untidiness, disorder, confusion . . . And what then? What is life to do to this heap of half-battered existence which they call their communion and which they would gladly call their happiness, if it were possible, and their future? Thus each loses himself for the sake of the other and loses the other and many others that wanted still to come. And loses the expanses and the possibilities, exchanges the approach and flight of gentle, divining things for an unfruitful perplexity out of which nothing can come save a little disgust, disillusionment, and poverty, and rescue in one of the many conventions that have been put up in large number like public refuges along the most dangerous road.[54]

In the penultimate paragraph of the letter, Rilke defines love itself as consisting in this: "that two solitudes protect and border and greet one another."[55]

This is no more an indictment of love per se than is a complaint about doggerel a rejection of poetry (although it does hold lovers up to what some might consider an impossibly high standard). It is rather an angry and disappointed prophet's violent denunciation of the perversions of something as supremely important as the source of our very identity (we are constituted by what we love—mountain landscapes, other persons, bottles of wine, or what you will), and the bond that unites us to the larger world around us, possibly expanding our consciousness of what life has to give, and making possible our highest and best accomplishments, which are (often enough) the fruit of our more solitary hours (novels aren't written at cocktail parties). Failing in love is not like failing to bake a cake, or to measure a plot of land properly; it is more like failing in the task of living well, or failing to become who we are. And, paradoxically, the forms of communion we seek as though they constituted highest bliss and the fulfillment of our deepest and most pervasive longings are, for the poet, little more than obstacles, contractions, and diversions; and what's worse, we baptize our failures with the names of "truth," "propriety," and "happiness" and are startled and unsettled when the knot loosens, and we find ourselves unhappy, and alone: "No one would ever dream of expecting a single individual to be happy—once someone is married, however, everyone is astonished that he is not."[56]

This is a constant refrain in the poetic condensation of the *Elegies*, but especially in the first three poems in the cycle, as the poet moves toward the outbreak of disgust mingled with sympathy and a scrap of transcendence in the "Fifth Elegy."

In the "First Elegy"—which lays out the topics and problems to be explored in what remains of the cycle, and gestures toward a solution, born of the "barren numbness" and the emptiness of significant loss, in the remarkable closing lines—(requited) lovers ("satisfied and stilled"), set in sharp contrast to the poet's beloved abandoned ones, merely "conceal in each other their lot."

The theme is picked up and expanded in the "Second Elegy," in an intimate address to the lovers themselves, in the cycle's most powerful portrayal of one of love's more lasting illusions, and the loss of self characteristic of a certain form of erotic abandonment. It is worth quoting (almost) in full, if only because it gives elaborate voice to Rilke's enduring anxiety about human sexuality:

> Lovers, gratified in each other, I ask you
> about us. You seize each other. Have you proof?
> Look, sometimes it happens that my hands come

to sense each other or my worn-out face
seeks shelter within them. That gives me a slight
sensation. But who would dare to *be* just for this?
But you who expand in the other's delight until,
overpowered, he begs you:
no *more*—; you who beneath his hands
swell like grapes on a harvest-year's vines;
you who often vanish, merely because another
spreads over you: I'm asking you about us. I know,
you touch so blissfully, because the caress endures,
because the place you so tenderly cover doesn't
vanish; because beneath it you feel
pure duration. So you promise eternity, almost,
from the embrace. And yet, when you've endured
the terrible first glances and the longing at the window,
and the first walk together, once only, through the garden:
lovers, *are* you the same? When you lift yourselves up
to each other's mouth and begin—drink against drink:
Oh how strangely the drinker flees from his action.

The images here are largely poetic figures of merely physical lovemak-
ing and gratification: swelling "like grapes on a harvest-year's vines"
recalls the aroused breast, the vanishing of the beloved when "another
spreads over" her is transparent enough. This is the true poetic indictment
of *fucking* that Hass locates, perhaps mistakenly, in the final stanza of
the "Fifth Elegy."[57] The error these lovers make is to believe that physical
contact—the caress, the kiss, copulation—promises eternity, or at least
"pure duration." Mostly, Rilke seems to be suggesting, it is two individuals losing themselves in the keen sentiments of bodily friction. But if *that*
is what lovers ultimately seek, why not simply touch oneself in solitude?
"That gives me a slight / sensation. But who would dare to *be* just for
this?"

This sort of loving embrace, which seems to promise release from time,
is merely another confirmation of the burden of being a fugitive among
apparently more solid and substantial *things*; and far from expanding
human consciousness toward the larger cosmic spaces of human existence, it seems only to contract the lover into a solitary point of unfruitful
sexual excitement and satiety. The outreaching and the enduring here
are spurious: mere sexual desire, satisfied and temporarily stilled, renews
itself, as every bodily desire does, but its satisfactions, divorced from the
larger world of our highest aspirations, remain eternally and depressingly

the same. When we set this sort of lover alongside Gaspara Stampa (the deserted sixteenth-century lover from Milan who went on to write a number of sonnets), it almost seems as though this form of engagement with another were meant to preclude involvement in and with the larger, more terrifying world we must somehow learn to love. As Rilke, anticipating, already asks in the "First Elegy":

> Isn't it time for us to free ourselves
> lovingly from the beloved and, tremblingly, to endure:
> as the arrow endures the bow, gathering itself to surpass itself
> in the tension of imminent release.

The "Third Elegy" begins to explore the larger (interior, archaic) landscape of (masculine) *erôs*, "lord of desire," which the lovers of the "Second Elegy" fail to reach—calls it "the deeply hidden, guilty river-god of the blood." Its theme is the domain of the *unconscious*, or that obscure place where consciousness and self-consciousness merge into blood; and its abiding question is: where does human consciousness, where this means *loving* consciousness, begin? If the *Elegies* as a whole are searching for home—a "strip of our own fruitful land, something human, / between stream and stone"—the "Third Elegy" begins to probe the inner tabernacle as a possible dwelling place, and examines, tentatively, its initially dark wild landscape and "surging chaos." (Here, too, the reader must rest content with a few pointers.)

At times the tone remains scornful, and chiding, especially in the first two sections: the young man, whom his beloved knows "only from afar," is an ignorant lover, estranged from the "unfathomable depths" of his desire, and the larger cosmic designs and dimensions (the "pure constellations") that form the model of his beloved's visage (the stars and constellations will return in the affirmative "Seventh" and "Tenth" elegies,); the young compassionate girl mistakenly believes that she alone is the source of his heart's trembling, and the "disquieting shock" of "more ancient terrors"; and his mother is accused—and it is a serious accusation in the mouth of *this* poet—of making her son small in beginning him, and holding at bay "things unfamiliar," when he might have been released fruitfully into the unknown; and so, in images of sidestepping, contraction, and conformity, by virtue of her "gentle presence" his "fate stepped behind the wardrobe," and his "restless future conformed itself to the folds of the curtain." Here, with scornful brevity, the poet seems to be telling us how we come to inhabit the interpreted world of the "First Elegy," how the world, strange at first because new, comes to seem familiar, and assumes the shape of our *first* habitation, where we are not, despite appearances, truly at home.

But consciousness is also in touch with deeper and larger forces, whether we know it or not. Dreaming, the boy surrenders to "floods of origin welling up within him." And for a season he surrenders to "his inwardness, his interior wilderness."

We *think*, in loving and seeking home, that we are reaching out toward *this* particular individual; but the elegy undercuts our confidence. We are not at home in loving; no more, at least, than we are in the interpreted world. Beneath the crust of civilization and culture, there are dark drives we cannot fully understand—the point where the human makes contact with nature, or rediscovers buried sources of its movements, presented in the first stanza in the mythical figure of Neptune "and his terrifying trident." And in a remarkable poetic echoing of Diotima's speech in the *Symposium*, in partial praise of philandering as a necessary stage in the soul's growth, the poet warns that the true lover loves "not just someone still to come, but a / measureless gathering" and "the entire / soundless landscape under a clouded or / pure destiny—; *this*, dear girl, came before you."

And yet, the poet does not appear to celebrate wildness for its own sake, but only, perhaps, as fruitful *beginning*. Already in the opening stanza, as we saw, Rilke speculates that the lover's delight in the face of the beloved stems from the *stars* (ancient symbol of purity, constancy, sublimation); and while "an immemorial sap" and a measureless gathering of beloveds, fathers and mothers and an "entire soundless landscape" come always before *this one here*, the poem ends with the following words of advice to the (female) lover: "lead him / close to the garden, and give him what outweighs / the night . . . . . . / Restrain him . . . . . ." Here, the cultivated plot replaces the wild and dark night, where boundaries and borders dissolve, and all things grow indistinct in our perceptions. If we wanted to condense the task in a mythical figure, we could say, stealing from Nietzsche: Dionysus must bear the yoke of Apollo.

A larger arena opens up, then, beneath and beyond the surface of our loves, a playing field as large as life or being itself, and as powerful as anything we *can* know. We are implicated in it, regardless of what we know and can say explicitly about it, and it moves us and influences us, often without our knowing complicity. Our greatest struggles are evidence of a love affair with nothing less than the world (of what we call, in our darker moments, "fate"—when it upsets our hopes and unsettles our confidence); and the source of our greatest dissatisfactions with what the world has to give seems to be the partiality of our attachments and romantic commitments, which promise so much and so often leave us disappointed, discouraged, and in despair.

We expect in a lover "distance, hunting, and home," but barely approach one another's borders, and finally fail to wonder what's on the other side. We play at parting and farewell in a "familiar garden," costumed and made up for the role, serious enough, and go back to our apartments like a bourgeois and enter the dreariness of everyday life through the kitchen. We sometimes set out to conquer the entire world in our youth, and find ourselves filling out forms behind a desk to scratch out a living, and looking to our children to accomplish what we didn't, or couldn't, or whipping ourselves up into spurious enthusiasm in times of carnival, or attending church, "clean and pure but disappointing like a post office on Sunday." And we complain, in rare moments, perhaps, of the terrible *unreality* of life and the world as we know it: time and the world can seem our greatest enemies, and death which marks their limit and so gives them shape.

The World Within

We have, each of us, our list of grievances and reasons for denial and the scornful retreat. Illness incurable and unsolicited rises often to the top, followed by death of the beloved or betrayal, divorce, and untimely loss of faculty. War and the constant readiness for war will enter some ranks; poverty, humiliation, and professional failure quarrel for their rightful place. Nature's inhospitality is irksome, at the very least, but so too the liar's successes and the honest man's grief, the triumph of what passes for vice, the spread of indifference and narcissism, withering affection, loneliness, coldness, hatred and faction, to speak in the preacher's vein. The trivial deserves a hearing as well, the wart disfiguring an otherwise lovely face, being too tall or short, a cracked piece of cherished crystal, the yellowed, crumbling pages of an old, important book. And there's the awful brevity of even the happiest of lives, which trumps the Epicurean's consoling thought. And above all, and more generally: a world that takes away as much as it gives. We throw everything in imagined scales, sad and heavyweight against light cause for joy, and pronounce our nay-saying verdict. In light of our common ideals, the world stands often enough condemned, if only for failing to give us what we want. In the calculating frame of mind, defended by Socrates in the *Protagoras* (where utilitarianism may be said to begin, but not without irony), being here is anything but glorious: "Each torpid turning of the world has its disinherited ones, / to whom neither the earlier nor what's about to come truly belongs."

Rilke's final affirmation of human life in the *Elegies* takes its stand within that obscure region where will and world meet, or where vision and landscape, subject and object, find occasion to greet one another and manage somehow to cohere, against our *wooing* expectations. It can be a fleeting reconciliation, "for an hour, or perhaps not even for an hour," when one finds oneself unaccountably "at one with a true measure of time scarcely / measurable between two moments" and filled with "a sense of being." It can unfold with the forces of the natural world over "a purely affirmative day" in summer, from dawn to dusk, "but equally the nights!" And there is love, which, as we've seen, is arguably the poet's lasting problem. One can, it seems, speak of it always only indirectly, in tropes and metaphors and parables. Schelling called the site where this reconciling affirmation takes place "the point of indifference." But what happens there, wherever it is, is anything but indifferent.

It falls to the "Seventh" and "Ninth" elegies to name this space or place, where this means to give it *poetic* voice. In the "Seventh," where the breakthrough itself is announced, the accent appears to fall on the subject and that "invisible realm within us" where the things we've come to love, and often to lose, *may* take up their proper residence, where the "extravagances of the heart" in an affirmative frame of mind spread themselves out and, with the poet's help and *Herz-Werk*,[58] more monumentally endure. In a poem dated August 1914, two years after the long work on the *Elegies* began, Rilke names it, pregnantly and ambiguously, "the world's inner space" (*Weltinnenraum*). But what are we to make of what Blanchot aptly describes as "this interiority of the exterior" and, as I prefer to add, this exteriority of the interior?[59]

It is, I think, too easy to saddle the poet with what Heidegger often calls in an indicting turn of phrase the "metaphysics of subjectivity," if this means, to paraphrase and condense the longer argument, an account that places the subject of representation and willing at the center of reality, at the expense of a world the subject is bent from the start on mastering. Rilke's poetry often pits itself against a view of human life that envisions the human task in terms of mastery and possession in the modern terms staked out by Bacon and Descartes, among others. The "Eighth Elegy's" ambiguous celebration of the Open takes its stand against the philosophical privilege of representation (*Vorstellung*), the face-to-face of subject and object, and the project of mastering life and world on Cartesian terms.

We'd come closer, I think, to the truth about the inward space and the heart-work so dear to the poet if we abandoned misleading talk of consciousness and self-consciousness, subjectivity and the subject—I take Rilke to have achieved a hard-won overcoming of merely subjective poetry, Romantic in the worst sense, during the period of the so-called thing-poems—and spoke instead of the task of attuning ourselves to the things of this world that call for something like poetic redemption and affirmation, as if to say: the world grows with us as we struggle to give it sense and flesh and word. It is true that Rilke tends to capture his sense of the task in terms of consciousness—although sometimes, perhaps surprisingly (see the letter to Hulewicz), in the language of intensified and expanded consciousness—but always in a way that includes reference to world and the meaning and "superior significances" we body forth in language in relation to world, or with a view toward what Blanchot calls the world's "higher and more demanding meanings."[60]

Here I take my leave once again from Heidegger, an otherwise congenial companion in the philosopher's quest to make room for poetry, and in keeping with Michel Haar's conviction that "Heidegger oversimplifies and dissimulates the fundamental themes of Rilke's thought more than he elucidates them."[61] Haar argues, more specifically, that while Rilke belongs to the age of subjectivity (we all do, even by Heidegger's own lights), his poetry is not obviously consistent with the role assigned to the subject by Descartes and his successors, including Kant, Fichte, and Hegel. I think that Rilke recognized, as well as Heidegger, that important things don't just happen in one's head, so to speak, although what we make of them, when we speak about them, surely matters. Again, Michel Haar seems to me to get Rilke's poetic ventures into the world within right, in the form of a rhetorical question: "Must we not admit even in the simplest approach to things, in vision, that the density, the innermost 'substance' and the inaccessibility of space, is what inhabits us?" Again: "Rilke recognizes in the 'inside' the characteristics of the 'outside,' and in the 'outside' the powers of an 'inside.' "[62] And finally: "Everywhere there is exchange, circulation of the interior and the exterior."[63] Where *I* am, or wherever the lyric poet discovers himself and his inner resources and visions, the world is, too: *Wo Es war, soll Ich werden.* (More on this in the next section, which completes or, more modestly, complements these short remarks on interiority.)

The world, paraphrasing Thoreau, constantly and obediently embodies our conceptions of it. *How* the world is there, for each of us, cannot be cleanly separated from how we stand in the midst of the world; whether the world presents a cheerful visage or wears a melancholy countenance tells us as much about ourselves as it reveals what's out there. Once we renounce the idea of a world behind the scenes which imposes itself upon us, and *decides* for us how it will be taken up and construed, whether lovingly or in denial, it seems natural enough to look for the very being or sense of what there is, and the possibility of affirming existence itself, in what we think and say about it, in how reality echoes and resonates in something like *interior* space: "Nowhere, dear one, will a world be but within us." Or in what, having made the world our own (rendered it "invisible" in Rilke's way of speaking), we say about it. As Heller shrewdly cautions us, be careful what you say about the world; it *is* like that.[64]

Saying Things

> And these things, which
> live by perishing, understand that you praise them; fleeting,
> they long for us to save them, us, the most fleeting of all.

Mind, then, is not some free-floating Cartesian substance, with content coming to itself from itself alone, as it disports with its own mental states and decides in advance what the realm of *res extensa* must be; mind is woven out of the very stuff of the world, bearing everywhere and always its mark. Barring severe dementia, which erases what passes within as quickly as it arrives, we *are* the accumulation of what the world with our help has made of us: internal space, the poet's fertile field, is formed in relation to what happens on the other side of the border—no outside, nothing inside. In the simple words of one of the poet's worthy precursors, *ein Gespräch sind wir* (we are a conversation).

If the world comes home in the mind of the receptive and grateful poet, it is still *the world* that settles—the seasons and the climate, birds, trees, mountains, lakes, day and night, friends and lovers, and "this darkly reticent earth." In a remarkable passage in Proust's *Within a Budding Grove* (quoted by Landy), the difficulty of deciding between the inner and the outer, or the fruitful exchange between what we conveniently divide, is wonderfully conveyed by the novel's narrator Marcel: "the better part of our memories exist outside us, in a blatter of rain, in the smell of an unaired room or of the first crackling brushwood fire in a cold grate. . . . Outside us? Within us, rather, but hidden from our eyes in an oblivion more or less prolonged."[65]

The price of saying "yes" to human life and our own experience of it would be too great if we had to renounce the world itself; and the result of taking leave would be, I venture to say, incoherent; or at least far from the promised affirmation of human life and everything that happens here.[66] The ontological stance sketched earlier too briefly and in strokes too broad, I confess, is at least nothing solipsistic, as the "Ninth Elegy," praising the earth and the poet's responsibility to what earthly existence has to give, makes very clear: "Earth, isn't this what you want: to arise within us, / *invisible*?" This will seem solipsistic, I think, if we still cling to the idea, canvassed earlier, that the earth is something that exists, and is what it is, beyond every effort to say what it means, and what it means to inhabit a world that sometimes resists our efforts to lend the things we encounter our voice. If I find myself moved, genuinely, by a setting sun, I should aspire to reproduce the experience in a world of words that does dusk some justice, as if the sunset were calling upon me to lend it a hand in speech. Provided I'm a poet, who cares to do justice in words to what matters, and so to praise and to memorialize in speech what I've experienced. To say that the earth *wants* to arise within us invisibly is just to say that the earth is something in some moments we find ourselves *loving*. As Michel Haar notes, defending Rilke against Heidegger, to say that the earth demands, or desires or *longs*, to be made invisible is just to say, possibly, that the earth comes home in the poem.[67] And it is at least worth noting, as Haar does against Heidegger, that the subject of the poetic statement, in both the grammatical sense and in the sense of agency, is *Earth* and not *I*. In a more phenomenological register, the line appears to suggest that certain of our experiences of the human world and earth demand a thoughtful, poetic way of taking them up. To find myself moved, genuinely moved, by a sunset, say, is not unlike feeling the pressure of a beloved to do the experience and its object justice. It strikes me that, in moments like this, it makes little sense to see, or to read, what I go on to say as an imposition, in words, upon a passive substrate.

What's at issue in Rilke's praise of interiority is what Lysaker calls the birth of sense, and the poetic conditions that make it possible for us to inhabit a *meaningful* world,[68] where this means—a world that *is*, in the original sense of what "being" means, before the thinning thought makes reality over in an image of non-sense, and we feel ourselves imprisoned in the poverty of our own *un*making. (It's worth at least recalling here that the poet is originally a *maker*, in this context helping to make *sense* of what Heidegger calls our "being-in-the-world.")

In a pregnant reversal of our common approach to the world, seeking happiness, or advantage, in mere circumstance and waiting for external events to give us what, enduringly, we want (and want to endure), the poet invites us to consider the world as calling *us* to come to its aid, asking for redemption in *our* vision and poetically attuned labor, and so as somehow needing us to bring it more fully and intensely into being. The world in the "Ninth Elegy" could almost be said to be wooing *us*. But we are too often looking to be loved and confirmed, by what's outside, that we are good enough, when we should be striving to become more capable and competent and worthy lovers of what existence, at once beautiful and terrifying, has to give.

Why be human, Rilke asks in the opening stanza. Not because happiness *is*, "that rashly snatched advantage in approaching loss," but because "being here is so much, and because everything / local apparently needs us, all those fugitive things that / oddly penetrate us . . . the most fugitive thing of all." The things that exist *are* vanishing, "more than ever." (Again, Marcel's ambivalence comes to mind: in *Swann's Way* we hear that "houses, roads, avenues are as fugitive, alas, as the years," but the subsequent course of the novel shows that these things can persist in the spaces of the poetic or literary endeavor.[69] Still, it's these things, and, admittedly, our having experienced them as well, that matter.) But we can praise them, and so rescue them in our pregnant utterances and poetic sayings from annihilating time and the oblivion of a past without a memorial to mark and preserve what is no more: for this *once and never again* is the law of each thing's being. Temples and cathedrals decay, natural things are born to die, and our most enduring accomplishments never remain the same as they migrate through the history of the world, almost as if, echoing Anaximander, they were doing penance for having come into being and *must* perish for stepping out of the void. We alone, it seems, are able to grasp the larger implications of the *never again*, and to make good on the transience of mortal things and the pain their passing brings to those who endure: "Perhaps we are *here* in order to say: house, / bridge, fountain, gate, pitcher, fruit tree, window—at most: column and tower. . . . but to *say*, understand, oh to say them *so* much more deeply than the things / themselves intended to be." Poetry is not therapy; or if it happens to be therapeutic, it isn't because it helps purge us of dangerous pent-up emotions, but (more beneficially) because it is the source of a reconciling ontology, where *things* are allowed to be what they are—meaningful, despite or even *because* fleeting and sometimes hard to endure:

> Our heart survives between the
> hammers, like the tongue
> between the teeth, and still, it
> somehow remains praising.

And in a remarkable stanza, worth quoting almost in full (if only because it condenses so beautifully so much of what the poet, or his lyrical persona, has come to see), Rilke suggests that our poetic work in *this* world of ours may just interest and amaze the angel himself, figure of transcendence and the unhappy longing for another order of being altogether:

> Praise the world to the angel, not the unsayable one,
> you cannot impress *him* with glorious feelings; in the universe
> where he feels more feelingly, you are a novice. So show
> him some simple thing, formed from generation to generation,
> which lives as our own, close to hand and in our sight.
> Speak to him of things. He will stand amazed, as you once did
> by the rope-maker in Rome or the potter near the Nile.
> Show him how happy a thing can be, and how innocent and ours,
> how even lamenting grief resolves purely to form itself,
> serves as a thing, or dies into a thing—and blissfully
> escapes beyond the violin.

We have, it seems, what these higher beings never will: a reason to deny, to be sure, but the chance to affirm, and in affirming to sing of a world of fragile beauty, rounded with a sleep, where *we* are the angel's tutors and counselors, and guides to what they can, with our help, hope but dimly to understand and admire: the reasons we often employ to justify escape from the world and denial of its value turn out to be the fructifying source of our most passionate *amor mundi*.

Platonism Revisited

> Yes: the more a person has recognized here, the more farewells
> he will have had to accomplish over the course of his life. But I
> often feel as if these partings would once again be affirmations
> in an open world where they would bear different names.
> —Rilke to Rudolf Burckhardt, April 14, 1924

In light of where we began, it seems fitting to return to Plato, if only briefly and in parting; for it is possible to interpret the poet's affirmative vision, or at least the sketch of it offered earlier, as an aesthetic variation on an old theme first broached in the *Symposium*, if only in the end to find it wanting. And it is possible as well to interpret the message of Plato's dialogue as more receptive to the values embedded in the experience of this world than a few of the dialogues would have one think, as we began to argue earlier. It would be misleading to claim or to imply that the *Republic*'s quarrel between the poet and the philosopher means to confront us with a simple alternative between *this* life and a world *beyond*. Plato himself, as we saw, attends to the details of scene and person and the earthly origin and motives of philosophic questioning in a way that suggests a this-worldly approach to philosophy, and a more affirmative vision of what this world has to offer. And there are poets whose dissatisfaction with the human condition, and desire to find some means of escape, rival Plato's, or compete with the views of one or more of his characters. Several of Plato's successors were at least as ambivalent as their master was about the value of embodied human experience. Plotinus's conflicted views on matter as both "non-being" and source of evil, a "decorated corpse," on the one hand, and as somehow participating in, or bearing traces of, the good, on the other, should give us pause before we offer impressionistic accounts of the choice between this world and another, in the work of Plato or in Rilke's poetry.[70]

The *Symposium* displays several important features that invite us to consider it in conclusion here. The framing narrative is unusually complex, and raises serious questions concerning Plato's commitment to direct philosophic speech and the value of straightforward argument, divorced from the occasions that prompt the philosophical account; and commentators more attuned to the dramatic structure of the dialogues have often found the framing narrative to be philosophically suggestive. The dialogue's complicated opening, full of rumors and uncertainty about when the affair took place, raise important questions concerning the problem of philosophic transmission and direct speech and argument. The one moment of what seems like authentic philosophic experience— Socrates alone on the neighbors' porch meditating—gives us nothing to think but only a figure to imagine, transfixed in thought. The dialogue includes an impressive roster of poets (Aristophanes and the lesser tragic poet Agathon) and lovers of poetry, whose views Plato artfully unfolds, and includes a lovely speech in praise of a certain conception of love which many today are likely to find convincing. Socrates himself attributes the position he goes on to defend, which seems to leave the territory of poetry's celebrations and grievings behind, to the Mantinean prophetess Diotima, in a speech rich in poetry and highly allusive: "what has been capable of making the aspiration to this 'higher' region live in our mind is the offspring of Plato the literary artist, who has brought us to this point scarcely by argument—rather by extended, subtly modulated rhetoric, layers of fictional narrators, and beguiling persuasion."[71] And at the dialogue's near end, Alcibiades gives a moving speech in praise of Socrates and his philosophical importance rich in imagery, and attuned to the particularity of human experience and the importance of the uniqueness of the person of Socrates himself. Among all the dialogues Plato left behind, it is the *Symposium* that makes one of the most convincing cases for the value of the poetic statement in the true lover's quest for wisdom; and the "ladder of love" that leads to the philosopher's otherworldly affirmations suggests no easy leap beyond the world of earthly particulars and into the blessed region of eternal forms, which Diotima herself describes and praises in a highly elusive, poetic vein.

The centerpiece, of course, is the view on love attributed to Diotima; and while I acknowledge that the speech attributed to her needs placing in a larger narrative context just outlined, I'll focus on the views associated with her here, if only to capture a strand in her conception of love that has proved most influential in the interpretation of the dialogue, and in a way that sheds light on what I take to be Rilke's affirmative stance toward human life in the *Elegies*.

Diotima's speech, like Rilke's *Elegies*, is a love story. The Mantinean prophet sings the praises of demonic *Eros*, born of Poros and Penia (Resource and Poverty), "tough, squalid, shoeless, and homeless, always lying on the ground without blanket or bed, sleeping in doorways and along waysides in the open air," ever in need, but always devising snares for "the beautiful and the good."[72] It is a parable, or a myth, meant to capture the source and soil of the kinetic aspect of the human condition, and to indicate a way out of our ignorance and unhappiness, where these are, or are argued elsewhere to be, one and the same. And like the *Phaedrus*, it places our particular (erotic) attachments to particular individuals (and times and places) in a more flattering light than the more political and impersonal vision of the *Republic* appears to allow. (The *Republic* is arguably about the importance, for certain political reasons, of living less personally, less poetically, and less attached to one's own, as the Straussians are wont to say.)

It is a story that begins in the midst of love's earthy, earthbound confusions, and all the feverish activity and creative turmoil that *Eros* introduces into the intelligent life of a dying animal, unsettled in time by intimations of immortality, and set in furious motion by passionate longing for the good it lacks but is compelled, by its very nature, to seek, and to secure *always* (*aei*). It is a story meant to illuminate the sense of urgency that attaches to our more serious endeavors (including childbearing, poetry, and lawmaking), and simultaneously to explain the insanity to which we often fall prey, in what resembles the uncanny disposition and antic behavior of the beasts in the heat of mating season. In Diotima's account, love proves to be desire for the lasting possession of what makes for highest bliss (hence the urgency). But we are the sorts of creatures who can be mistaken about the very object we invariably seek (hence the madness). The dialogue tries to do justice to both, or all three—the beginning and the end, and the stages and the temptations to get stuck in between.

Diotima's tale of love and its vicissitudes cannot explain the urgency or the pathology of our erotic lives without blazing a trail that leads from madness and inquietude to sanity and bliss, and comprehends along the way the striking diversity of what we mortals do in *one* undying underlying quest. From love of bodily beauty in this one *here and now*, the soul ascends, ideally, to the appreciation of bodily beauty *as such* (passing through a phase of beneficial philandering), to the love of a form that remains always what it is, beyond the decaying, perishing particular that fleetingly embodies it. On this plain the ideal lover will come to see that the beauty of corporeal shape is less noble than the beauty discernible, with effort, in souls and what mind strains to achieve, becoming a lover of our more active pursuits, and the laws we devise for the benefit of communing souls. From there, he may come to love the *knowledge* and insight that underwrite what, at our very best, we think and do and legislate. And finally, if all things conspire in our lover's favor, he'll come to see, in a sudden glimpse of the ultimate object of his longing, what is beautiful by nature, beyond existence itself, something "always being and neither coming to be nor perishing, nor increasing nor passing away," the single form of the beautiful *itself*, "alone by itself and with itself," which explains his interest in all the fleetingly beautiful things he (mistakenly or blindly or in a fit of passion) admired, before he entered the native realm of truth. "It is at this place in life, in beholding the beautiful itself . . . that [life] is worth living, if human life can be said to be worth living anywhere at all."[73]

When we finally realize what makes what we love *truly* lovable, we will achieve the untroubled happiness we dimly sought among the dying particulars we mistakenly loved and admired and recklessly pursued, and give birth to the genuine offspring of our communion with the beautiful and the good; and the evanescence of particulars, striving but failing to imitate a deathless model, will no longer trouble us. The course of true love unobstructed lifts us above the human condition, and places us on a peak, in rarefied air, where, looking down, human affairs and the confusions they breed are nothing short of contemptible, or silly; or, if we can find some reason to praise them, are the necessary stepping-stones to a vision from above that's left them behind and unmourned in their passing. It's tempting to see in her speech an epitome of Plato's ambiguity facing the poetic statement: a desire to do it justice as an anticipation of what the philosopher is supposed to know in other ways, and a sense that poetry, however moving, however thoughtful, however nourishing, cannot *know* what the philosopher is *said*, in an admittedly poetic gesture, to be able to perceive.

I refuse the easy gesture of dismissing Plato (or Socrates or his Mantinean tutor), and lack the strength of argument to refute Diotima's account, although my own sympathies side more frequently with the particulars the Platonizing movement *seems* willing at times to deny, or to read as stages in an ascent that leaves the particulars behind. For those who wish to rescue Plato (or Socrates or Diotima) from the charge of banishing the poets and their preoccupation with particular individuals, it is worth observing that poets find no unequivocal place in Diotima's depiction of the stages of the soul's journey up the ladder. She does include poets in her account of those who beget in the beautiful, although even here they take a back seat to legislators, but they do not appear to play any direct role in the upward path. Poets are compelling, it seems, only at the earliest stages of the ideal lover's projected ascent, when the love of bodies still commands assent and the particularities of the world we experience still govern our concern. At the higher levels, poetic discourse more or less disappears, accept insofar as Diotima herself can be said to be, throughout the account of the ladder of love, a poet herself. But, again, Plato himself is writing poetically here. And so we are left to wonder and should not leap to ready conclusions. We can be too eager to settle our affairs, although experience teaches caution and reluctance to offer a ready *yes* or *no* to the weightiest questions. My ambition is comparative and exploratory, and the reader must decide for herself where wisdom resides, or what Plato meant to say about poetry, philosophy, and love in the *Symposium*.

Rilke's world is itself a city of words, like Plato's, constructed against time to endure against approaching loss, and as a monument that outlives the fleeting experiences and objects that gave it birth. And it is rife with the language of conversion, a favored way of speaking about the philosophical life in the *Republic*, as if to say: the turning toward the right domain is the primal act, poetic or philosophic, that makes things right, beyond or before the work of reason (inward for Rilke, toward the ideas that do not wander in Plato's Socrates). It is born of a Platonic dissatisfaction with the evanescence of mortal things; and it excludes much of what Plato (or Socrates or Diotima) found contemptible in our normal erotic expectations, especially the Aristophanic image of fusion and completion in the imagined other half. The poet grounds his disappointment with what unlearned *erôs* accomplishes in an affirmative vision of the larger world the untutored lover designs his life to avoid, with or without awareness of what this designing means to accomplish. Like the Mantinean prophet of the *Symposium*, the author of the *Elegies* appears to trace out a path that leaves our particular attachments happily behind: "Be ahead of all parting," in the words of the *Sonnets to Orpheus*, and purify your dissatisfactions in the distillate of the poem.

Art, it seems, is larger and more lasting and hence more valuable than life itself, which serves merely as occasion for the poet's transcending constructions. We don't read Shakespeare in order to learn about particular individuals. Nor are we likely to care about the personal experience that gave rise to Tennyson's "In Memoriam." Hart Crane's "mustard scansion of the eyes" is probably not best interpreted as an account of the jaundiced, alcoholic poet's reading of the lines of his precursors. Poetry is a way of crystallizing and memorializing, or freezing or mummifying (as Nietzsche would say) something that would otherwise be consumed by the relentless flux of time, or fade, as most things do, into insignificance.

We are too often too ready to distinguish between thinkers who speak favorably of *being*, and those who appear to celebrate *becoming*; and to associate the latter with a life-affirming tendency, while saddling the former with an attitude hostile to life. Heraclitus, after all, is devoted to the enduring logos or the law of what becomes, against those who would fall back and into a more personal way of perceiving the world; and Parmenides tells a *story* of enduring and unchanging truth that appears to take seriously our being conditioned and *on the way* toward the better, because more truthful, vision of what is. Still, poets have a tendency to think of their work as somehow removed from the life that gave it birth, and not always to the latter's credit: "A thing is definite; the art object has to be even more definite; removed from all chance, freed of all uncertainty, lifted out of time and given to space, it has become lasting, capable of eternity."[74] We are here to *say* . . . . as if the world were redeemable *only* in speech, and came into being merely for the sake of writing undying poems: "Yet do thy worst, old time; despite thy wrong, / My love shall in my verse ever live young."[75]

For the sake of writing poems, and fancying that the world came to be for *his* sake, and now stands ready to answer to his calling: is this not the narcissism of the poet? But perhaps the question contains an ambiguity. We can ask why the world came into being looking back, in search of intelligence and design, perhaps, or in a scientific frame of mind, pursuing the chain of causes back to their dark and distant source, in an effort to explain what indifferently exists, as the necessary background of all we do. Or we can ask moving forward, in search of something worthwhile to do and to be, and measuring the world's existence in accordance with our highest vocation. Moving forward, as we *must*, what we see and how we see are shaped by what we take ourselves to be. This is why the poet and the industrialist, the lover and the nihilist, religious individuals and the non-religious, among others, can be said to live in different *worlds*, although in another sense, of course, they live always in the same world.

Rilke's is of course a poet's calling, which is to say that art gives body, form, and meaning to the very being of what there is: the world comes home to itself in the space of the poem, the meaning of what comes into being lives, somehow more fully, in its heightened artistic expression. "Art," the poet writes in 1909, "is not to be understood as a *selection* made of the world but as its entire transformation into magnificence."[76] What we're asking, then, is this: how does the world of particulars, which come and go, stand in the spaces of Rilke's art? Do they matter for their own sake? Or are they occasions for the transcending artistic gesture, and ingredients in a poetic alchemy that leaves its originals behind? Is this a legitimate dichotomy?

Platonism under some description, with or without the metaphysics Plato has often been saddled with, is probably unavoidable, if it is true that all of our speech acts include a generalizing moment. Words are not things; or if they are things of a sort, they are not one with their referent (the word "food" satisfies no one's hunger). Every speaking gesture and the labor of writing leave the particulars behind, even when we lend *this thing here and now* our voice.[77] I say "apple"—meaning what's before my very eyes—but the name carries me away toward something that endures beyond the fruit I now consume. I say "dinosaur" and mean something that no longer *is*, but that persists in the language and theory of contemporary science. As a novelist, I can build a world in speech that exists nowhere save in words. Lyric poems are things that exist on scraps of ephemeral paper, but their meaning lies elsewhere, and beyond the particular occasions that give them birth. Even proper names, once bestowed, can be bestowed again and again: I don't draw much closer to this particular individual by saying *Marie*. And everything I go on to say about Marie could be said, at least in principle, of anyone else. Every utterance is a parting gesture.

But there is more than one way to say "farewell" to what departs, and more than one variety of otherworldliness. We've already had occasion to note that the things of this world are always saying farewell, so to speak. The world, as we saw, takes away as much as it gives; and it is this fact, if not this fact alone, which drives the lyric poet to transcribe his questions and her loves in verse. Our passions die; our capacities wither; and our works are not guaranteed an audience beyond the day and the passing interests that gave them birth. The question is: how to be disposed toward and to speak of passing things? If Platonism names philosophical contempt for this world of evanescent things (the philosopher, estranged in his body, is always preparing for death, as we noted earlier), then Rilke's poetic ontology is an overcoming of Platonism, if not the more complex and ambiguous positions that come forward and compete with one another in Plato's own work. For the poet's ambition is nothing less than to celebrate *this* world in songs of praise, despite, or even because of, its tendency to disappoint our expectations, and to take aware as much as it gives; while most of those texts that have nourished the tradition of Platonism can be said to celebrate this world as an avenue to someplace else, in what often seems an ascetic frame of mind (again, the *Phaedo* stands out as one of the more eloquent sources of the ascetic strand among Platonists). "Asceticism," Rilke notes in 1921, "is no solution: it is sensuality with a negative prefix."[78] And shortly before his death of leukemia: "it is our task to impress this provisional, transient earth upon ourselves so deeply, so agonizingly, and so passionately that its essence rises up again 'invisibly' within us."[79]

As we saw in our discussion of Rilke's inward turn, on the one hand, coupled with his turn toward *things*, on the other, this need not be seen as a reversion to subjective metaphysics, but rather as a call to make our own, somehow, the significance—including the pain and the grief we experience facing loss—of those things we have the privilege to experience in a world that means best when we think and write about it in an appropriately attuned frame of mind. In the words of two early *Sonnets to Orpheus*: *Gesang ist Dasein*, and *Rühmen, das ists!* ("Song is being here," and "Praising, that's it!") And if our song is grieving, the poet implores us to remember: "Only in the realm of praising may Lament / move." "Be ahead of all parting," yes, but also, among fading and decaying things, "the glass that rings out as it's breaking."[80] Too often we "waste our pains. / How we glance beyond them, into woeful duration, / perhaps hoping for an end." But the sources of our misery are

> our preserving winter leaves, our dark sense of green,
> *one* season of the familiar year—not only a stretch
> of time—but place, settlement, camp, soil and dwelling.

Not to escape the human condition, then, but to live it as fully as we can, risking much, and to find reason to affirm it and to speak well, or poetically, about it, despite the terror and the misery and the disappointment—that is the Rilkean poet's task: "The most divine consolation is without a doubt contained within the human itself."[81]

It is possible, as we've seen, to complicate the otherworldly aspects of the Platonic dialogues, against a long-standing tradition of Platonic contempt for the world of human things, but it is difficult to imagine Socrates in Plato saying, in some Greek equivalent: *Hiersein ist herrlich*, "Being here is glorious," in the memorable words of the "Seventh Elegy," from which we've taken our volume's title.

The writings Plato left behind give powerful expression to that longing for a purer, stiller world than ours, the promise of a better world elsewhere, although the path that leads elsewhere is squarely rooted in things we find happening in this world. And the speech of Diotima in the *Symposium* traces a path of ascent, leading to highest bliss, if only we mortals could follow. Rilke, as we've seen, sometimes flirts with a qualified version of the Platonic aspiration. And, as I've tried to argue, or to show in several pregnant examples, Plato's dialogues often display a qualified version of this-worldliness.[82] But in the closing lines of the marvelous "Tenth Elegy," the poet announces, in a reversal of the mighty Platonic legacy (if not a reversal of Plato's own vision):

> But if the endlessly dead awakened in us a sign and symbol,
> look, they'd point, perhaps, to the catkins hanging from
> the empty hazels, or they'd
> intend the rain, falling onto the earth's dark soil in springtime—
>
> And we, who think of happiness
> *rising*, would sense the emotion,
> that almost dismays us,
> when a happy thing *falls*.

Part Two

✦

The Elegies

Duineser Elegien

Aus dem Besitz der Fürstin

Marie von Thurn und Taxis-Hohenlohe

(1912/1922)

Die erste Elegie

Wer, wenn ich schriee, hörte mich denn aus der Engel
Ordnungen? und gesetz selbst, es nähme
einer mich plötzlich ans Herz: ich verginge von seinem
stärkeren Dasein. Denn das Schöne ist nichts
als des Schrecklichen Anfang, den wir noch grade ertragen,
und wir bewundern es so, weil es gelassen verschmäht,
uns zu zerstören. Ein jeder Engel ist schrecklich.
   Und so verhalt ich mich denn und verschlucke den Lockruf
dunkelen Schluchzens. Ach, wen vermögen
wir denn zu brauchen? Engel nicht, Menschen nicht,
und die findigen Tiere merken es schon,
daß wir nicht sehr verläßlich zu Haus sind
in der gedeuteten Welt. Es bleibt uns vielleicht
irgend ein Baum an dem Abhang, daß wir ihn täglich
wiedersähen; es bleibt uns die Straße von gestern
und das verzogene Treusein einer Gewohnheit,
der es bei uns gefiel, und so blieb sie und ging nicht.
   O und die Nacht, die Nacht, wenn der Wind voller Weltraum
uns am Angesicht zehrt—, wem bliebe sie nicht, die ersehnte,
sanft enttäuschende, welche dem einzelnen Herzen
mühsam bevorsteht. Ist sie den Liebenden leichter?
Ach, sie verdecken sich nur mit einander ihr Los.
   Weißt du's *noch* nicht? Wirf aus den Armen die Leere
zu den Räumen hinzu, die wir atmen; vielleicht daß die Vögel
die erweiterte Luft fühlen mit innigerm Flug.

Ja, die Frühlinge brauchten dich wohl. Es muteten manche
Sterne dir zu, daß du sie spürtest. Es hob

Duino Elegies

From the Property of Princess
Maria von Thurn und Taxis-Hohenlohe
(1912/1922)

The First Elegy

Who, if I cried out, would hear me among the angels'
orders? and even if one of them took me
suddenly to heart: I would perish in its overwhelming
being. For beauty is merely
the beginning of terror, which we can barely endure,
and it makes us marvel, because it blithely refuses
to destroy us. Every angel is terrifying.
    And so I pull myself back and swallow the luring call
of dark sobbing. Ah, who answers to our
nameless need? Not angels, not humans,
and discovering animals already note
that we are not truly at home
in the interpreted world. Perhaps on a hillside
some tree remains for us, that we can see again,
daily; there remains for us yesterday's street
and the comforting loyalty of a habit
that stayed and settled in and would not leave us.
    Oh and night, the night, when wind filled with worldspace
tears at our faces—, for whom would it not remain, the gently
disillusioning object of longing, which the solitary heart
so painfully greets. Is it lighter for lovers?
But they only conceal in each other their lot.
    You *still* don't know? Cast the emptiness out of your
arms and into the spaces we breathe; perhaps in order for birds
to feel the expanded air with intensified flight.

Yes, the springtimes truly needed you. Sometimes the stars
looked to you to notice them. A wave

sich eine Woge heran im Vergangenen, oder
da du vorüberkamst am geöffneten Fenster,
gab eine Geige sich hin. Das alles war Auftrag.
Aber bewältigtest du's? Warst du nicht immer
noch von Erwartung zerstreut, als kündigte alles
eine Geliebte dir an? (Wo willst du sie bergen,
da doch die großen fremden Gedanken bei dir
aus und ein gehn und öfters bleiben bei Nacht.)
Sehnt es dich aber, so singe die Liebenden; lange
noch nicht unsterblich genug ist ihr berühmtes Gefühl.
Jene, du neidest sie fast, Verlassenen, die du
so viel liebender fandst als die Gestillten. Beginn
immer von neuem die nie zu erreichende Preisung;
denk: es erhält sich der Held, selbst der Untergang war ihm
nur ein Vorwand, zu sein: seine letzte Geburt.
Aber die Liebenden nimmt die erschöpfte Natur
in sich zurück, als wären nicht zweimal die Kräfte,
dieses zu leisten. Hast du der Gaspara Stampa
denn genügend gedacht, daß irgend ein Mädchen,
dem der Geliebte entging, am gesteigerten Beispiel
dieser Liebenden fühlt: daß ich würde wie sie?
Sollen nicht endlich uns diese ältesten Schmerzen
fruchtbarer werden? Ist es nicht Zeit, daß wir liebend
uns vom Geliebten befrein und es bebend bestehn:
wie der Pfeil die Sehne besteht, um gesammelt im Absprung
mehr zu sein als er selbst. Denn Bleiben ist nirgends.

Stimmen, Stimmen. Höre, mein Herz, wie sonst nur
Heilige hörten: daß sie der riesige Ruf
aufhob vom Boden; sie aber knieten,
Unmögliche, weiter und achtetens nicht:
So waren sie hörend. Nicht, daß du *Gottes* ertrügest
die Stimme, bei weitem. Aber das Wehende höre,
die ununterbrochene Nachricht, die aus Stille sich bildet.
Er rauscht jetzt von jenen jungen Toten zu dir.
Wo immer du eintratst, redete nicht in Kirchen
zu Rom und Neapel ruhig ihr Schicksal dich an?
Oder es trug eine Inschrift sich erhaben dir auf,
wie neulich die Tafel in Santa Maria Formosa.
Was sie mir wollen? leise soll ich des Unrechts

arose to greet you from your own past, or
as you came toward an open window,
a violin gave itself freely. All this was mission.
But could you bear it? Weren't you always
distracted by expectation, as if everything
announced a beloved? (Where can you shelter
her, with those vast strange thoughts within you
coming and going and often staying the night.)
But when you long, sing of those who love; for
their famous feeling is still not undying enough.
You almost envy the deserted ones whom you found
all the more endearing than the satisfied and stilled.
Begin ever freshly the unattainable praising;
think: the hero endures, even his own downfall was
merely an excuse to give birth to himself again.
But Nature, exhausted, takes its lovers back into itself,
as though it hadn't the strength to accomplish this work
a second time. Have you remembered Gaspara Stampa
deeply enough, so that any girl abandoned by her beloved
might, by this more spirited example of loving, gradually
come to feel: that I could become like her?
Shouldn't these most ancient of sufferings finally bear
more fruit for us? Isn't it time for us to free ourselves
lovingly from the beloved and, tremblingly, to endure:
as the arrow endures the bow, gathering itself to surpass itself
in the tension of imminent release. Remaining is nowhere.

Voices, voices. Listen, my heart, as only saints
have listened: until the vast, terrible call
carried them away; but they kept on kneeling
impossibly and noticed nothing further:
So intently were they listening. Not that you could bear *God's*
voice, far from it. But listen to the murmuring of the wind,
and the unbroken message that forms itself of silence.
It rushes toward you now from those who died young.
Whenever you entered a church in Naples or Rome,
didn't their fate quietly approach to speak to you?
Or else an inscription carried you above yourself,
like the tablet lately in Santa Maria Formosa.
What do they want of me? Perhaps to remove gently

Anschein abtun, der ihrer Geister
reine Bewegung manchmal ein wenig behindert.

Freilich ist es seltsam, die Erde nicht mehr zu bewohnen,
kaum erlernte Gebräuche nicht mehr zu üben,
Rosen, und andern eigens versprechenden Dingen
nicht die Bedeutung menschlicher Zukunft zu geben;
das, was man war in unendlich ängstlichen Händen,
nicht mehr zu sein, und selbst den eigenen Namen
wegzulassen wie ein zerbrochenes Spielzeug.
Seltsam, die Wünsche nicht weiterzuwünschen. Seltsam,
alles, was sich bezog, so lose im Raume
flattern zu sehen. Und das Totsein ist mühsam
und voller Nachholn, daß man allmählich ein wenig
Ewigkeit spürt.—Aber Lebendige machen
alle den Fehler, daß sie zu stark unterscheiden.
Engel (sagt man) wüßten oft nicht, ob sie unter
Lebenden gehn oder Toten. Die ewige Strömung
reißt durch beide Bereiche alle Alter
immer mit sich und übertönt sie in beiden.

Schließlich brauchen sie uns nicht mehr, die Früheentrückten,
man entwöhnt sich des Irdischen sanft, wie man den Brüsten
milde der Mutter entwächst. Aber wir, die so große
Geheimnisse brauchen, denen aus Trauer so oft
seliger Fortschritt entspringt—: *könnten* wir sein ohne sie?
Ist die Sage umsonst, daß einst in der Klage um Linos
wagende erste Musik dürre Erstarrung durchdrang;
daß erst im erschrockenen Raum, dem ein beinah göttlicher Jüngling
plötzlich für immer enttrat, die Leere in jene
Schwingung geriet, die uns jetzt hinreißt und tröstet und hilft.

the appearance of injustice that sometimes
slightly hinders their souls from moving more purely.

It is truly strange to dwell on earth no longer,
no longer to practice customs one barely learned,
no longer to give roses and other promising things
the more expansive meaning of a human future;
no longer to be what one was in infinitely anxious
hands, to leave behind even one's own name
as quickly as a child abandons a broken toy.
Strange, no longer to wish one's wishes. Strange,
to see everything once related scattered so
loosely in space. And being dead is hard work
and full of retrieval, before one gradually senses
a little eternity.—But the living all make
the mistake of distinguishing too sharply.
Angels (they say) often don't know whether they move
among the living or the dead. The eternal current
always sweeps all ages through both realms
along with itself and resounds more loudly in both.

In the end, the early departed no longer need us,
they are weaned from the earth gently, as one
outgrows the mother's mild breast. But we,
who need such great mysteries, for whom grief is often
the blessed source of growth—*could* we be without them?
Is it an empty legend, that in the lament for Linos
the first music daringly pierced the barren numbness;
that in the startled space which a nearly godlike youth
suddenly left forever, the emptiness first felt
the vibration that now enraptures us and comforts and helps.

Die zweite Elegie

Jeder Engel ist schrecklich. Und dennoch, weh mir,
ansing ich euch, fast tödliche Vögel der Seele,
wissend um euch. Wohin sind die Tage Tobiae,
da der Strahlendsten einer stand an der einfachen Haustür,
zur Reise ein wenig verkleidet und schon nicht mehr furchtbar;
(Jüngling dem Jüngling, wie er neugierig hinaussah).
Träte der Erzengel jetzt, der gefährliche, hinter den Sternen
eines Schrittes nur nieder und herwärts; hochauf-
schlagend erschlüg uns das eigene Herz. Wer seid ihr?

Frühe Geglückte, ihr Verwöhnten der Schöpfung,
Höhenzüge, morgenrötliche Grate
aller Erschaffung,—Pollen der blühenden Gottheit,
Gelenke des Lichtes, Gänge, Treppen, Throne,
Räume aus Wesen, Schilde aus Wonne, Tumulte
stürmisch entzückten Gefühls und plötzlich, einzeln,
Spiegel: die die entströmte eigene Schönheit
wiederschöpfen zurück in das eigene Antlitz.

Denn wir, wo wir fühlen, verflüchtigen; ach wir
atmen uns aus und dahin; von Holzglut zu Holzglut
geben wir schwächern Geruch. Da sagt uns wohl einer:
ja, du gehst mir ins Blut, dieses Zimmer, der Frühling
füllt sich mit dir . . . Was hilfts, er kann uns nicht halten,
wir schwinden in ihm und um ihn. Und jene, die schön sind,
o wer hält sie zurück? Unaufhörlich steht Anschein
auf in ihrem Gesicht und geht fort. Wie Tau von dem Frühgras
hebt sich das Unsre von uns, wie die Hitze von einem
heißen Gericht. O Lächeln, wohin? O Aufschaun:
neue, warme, entgehende Welle des Herzens—;
weh mir: wir *sinds* doch. Schmeckt denn der Weltraum,
in den wir uns lösen, nach uns? Fangen die Engel
wirklich nur Ihriges auf, ihnen Entströmtes,
oder ist manchmal, wie aus Versehen, ein wenig
unseres Wesens dabei? Sind wir in ihre
Züge soviel nur gemischt wie das Vage in die Gesichter
schwangerer Frauen? Sie merken es nicht in dem Wirbel
ihrer Rückkehr zu sich. (Wie sollten sie's merken.)

The Second Elegy

Every angel is terrifying. And yet, alas,
I sing to you, almost deadly birds of the soul,
knowing about you. Where are the days of Tobias,
when one of the most radiant stood at a lowly doorstep,
slightly disguised for the journey and no longer dreadful;
(Like a young man gazing curiously at another youth).
If the archangel now, dangerously, from behind the stars
took a single step down toward us, our own rising heart
would pound us down to dust. Who are you?

Early successes, creation's spoiled offspring,
mountain ranges, ridges red with the dawn
of all desire,—pollen of the flowering godhead,
hinges of light, hallways, stairways, thrones,
spaces of essence, shields of ecstasy, tempests
of feeling, stormy and enraptured, then suddenly alone,
mirrors: gathering their own outpouring beauty
back into their untroubled faces again.

But we, when we feel, evaporate; alas, we breathe
ourselves out and away; from ember to ember
our fragrance grows fainter. Though someone tells us:
"Yes, you've entered my blood, this room, the spring
is filled with you . . ." It doesn't help, he can't hold us,
we vanish within and around him. And the beautiful ones,
who holds them back? Appearance rises endlessly
in their face and moves on. Like dew from the morning grass,
what is ours rises from us, like the heat from a hot dish
of food. O smile, where are you going? Uplifted glance:
new warm departing wave of the heart—;
alas: we *are* this. Does the worldspace we dissolve into
taste of us then? Do the angels really take back
only what pours out of themselves, or
sometimes, as if by oversight, is there a little
of our essence as well? Do we mingle in
with their features at least as much as vagueness in the faces
of pregnant women? They don't notice it in their whirling
return to themselves. (How could they notice it.)

Liebende könnten, verstünden sie's, in der Nachtluft
wunderlich reden. Denn es scheint, daß uns alles
verheimlicht. Siehe, die Bäume *sind*; die Häuser,
die wir bewohnen, bestehn noch. Wir nur
ziehen allem vorbei wie ein luftiger Austausch.
Und alles ist einig, uns zu verschweigen, halb als
Schande vielleicht und halb als unsägliche Hoffnung.

Liebende, euch, ihr in einander Genügten,
frag ich nach uns. Ihr greift euch. Habt ihr Beweise?
Seht, mir geschiehts, daß meine Hände einander
inne werden oder daß mein gebrauchtes
Gesicht in ihnen sich schont. Das giebt mir ein wenig
Empfindung. Doch wer wagte darum schon zu *sein* ?
Ihr aber, die ihr im Entzücken des andern
zunehmt, bis er euch überwältigt
anfleht: nicht *mehr*—; die ihr unter den Händen
euch reichlicher werdet wie Traubenjahre;
die ihr manchmal vergeht, nur weil der andre
ganz überhand nimmt: euch frag ich nach uns. Ich weiß,
ihr berührt euch so selig, weil die Liebkosung verhält,
weil die Stelle nicht schwindet, die ihr, Zärtliche,
zudeckt; weil ihr darunter das reine
Dauern verspürt. So versprecht ihr euch Ewigkeit fast
von der Umarmung. Und doch, wenn ich der ersten
Blicke Schrecken besteht und die Sehnsucht am Fenster,
und den ersten gemeinsamen Gang, *ein* Mal durch den Garten:
Liebende, *seid* ihrs dann noch? Wenn ihr einer dem andern
euch an den Mund hebt und ansetzt—: Getränk an Getränk:
o wie entgeht dann der Trinkende seltsam der Handlung.

Erstaunte euch nicht auf attischen Stelen die Vorsicht
menschlicher Geste? war nicht Liebe und Abschied
so leicht auf die Schultern gelegt, als wär es aus anderm
Stoffe gemacht als bei uns? Gedenkt euch der Hände,
wie sie drucklos beruhen, obwohl in den Torsen die Kraft steht.
Diese Beherrschten wußten damit: so weit sind wirs,
dieses ist unser, uns *so* zu berühren; stärker
stemmen die Götter uns an. Doch dies ist Sache der Götter.

Lovers, if they knew how, might speak wonderfully
in the night air. For it seems that everything
hides us. Look, the trees *are*; the houses
we dwell in still stand. We alone
fly past all things, like an airy exchange.
And everything unites to keep quiet about us,
half in shame perhaps, half as unsayable hope.

Lovers, gratified in each other, I ask you
about us. You seize each other. Have you proof?
Look, sometimes it happens that my hands come
to sense each other or my worn-out face
seeks shelter within them. That gives me a slight
sensation. But who would dare to *be* just for this?
But you who expand in the other's delight until,
overpowered, he begs you:
no *more*—; you who beneath his hands
swell like grapes on a harvest-year's vines;
you who often vanish, merely because another
spreads over you: I'm asking you about us. I know,
you touch so blissfully, because the caress endures,
because the place you cover so tenderly doesn't
vanish; because beneath it you feel
pure duration. So you promise eternity, almost,
from the embrace. And yet, when you've endured
the terrible first glances and the longing at the window,
and the first walk together, *once* only, through the garden:
lovers, *are* you the same? When you lift yourselves up
to each other's mouth and begin—: drink against drink:
Oh how strangely the drinker flees from his action.

Weren't you astonished by the caution of human gesture
on Attic steles? Weren't love and farewell
laid so lightly on the shoulders, as though formed
of different stuff than ours? Remember the hands,
how gently they rested, though there's power in the torsos.
These self-contained ones knew: we can go this far,
this is ours, to touch no further; the gods
press down harder upon us. But that's the gods' affair.

Fänden auch wir ein reines, verhaltenes, schmales
Menschliches, einen unseren Streifen Fruchtlands
zwischen Strom und Gestein. Denn das eigene Herz übersteigt uns
noch immer wie jene. Und wir können ihm nicht mehr
nachschaun in Bilder, die es besänftigen, noch in
göttliche Körper, in denen es größer sich mäßigt.

If only we, too, could find a pure, contained, slender
strip of our own fruitful land, something human,
between stream and stone. For our own heart exceeds us,
as theirs did. But we can no longer gaze after it
in soothing images or in godlike bodies,
where it measures itself in greater repose.

Die dritte Elegie

Eines ist, die Geliebte zu singen. Ein anderes, wehe,
jenen verborgenen schuldigen Fluß-Gott des Bluts.
Den sie von weitem erkennt, ihren Jüngling, was weiß er
selbst von dem Herren der Lust, der aus dem Einsamen oft,
ehe das Mädchen noch linderte, oft auch als wäre sie nicht,
ach, von welchem Unkenntlichen triefend, das Gotthaupt
aufhob, aufrufend die Nacht zu unendlichem Aufruhr.
O des Blutes Neptun, o sein furchtbarer Dreizack.
O der dunkele Wind seiner Brust aus gewundener Muschel.
Horch, wie die Nacht sich muldet und höhlt. Ihr Sterne,
stammt nicht von euch des Liebenden Lust zu dem Antlitz
seiner Geliebten? Hat er die innige Einsicht
in ihr reines Gesicht nicht aus dem reinen Gestirn?

Du nicht hast ihm, wehe, nicht seine Mutter
hat ihm die Bogen der Braun so zur Erwartung gespannt.
Nicht an dir, ihn fühlendes Mädchen, an dir nicht
bog seine Lippe sich zum fruchtbarern Ausdruck.
Meinst du wirklich, ihn hätte dein leichter Auftritt
also erschüttert, du, die wandelt wie Frühwind?
Zwar du erschrakst ihm das Herz; doch ältere Schrecken
stürzten in ihm bei dem berührenden Anstoß.
Ruf ihn . . . du rufst ihn nicht ganz aus dunkelem Umgang.
Freilich, er *will*, er entspringt; erleichtert gewöhnt er
sich in dein heimliches Herz und nimmt und beginnt sich.
Aber begann er sich je?
Mutter, *du* machtest ihn klein, du warsts, die ihn anfing;
dir war er neu, du beugtest über die neuen
Augen die freundliche Welt und wehrtest der fremden.
Wo, ach, hin sind die Jahre, da du ihm einfach
mit der schlanken Gestalt wallendes Chaos vertratst?
Vieles verbargst du ihm so; das nächtlich-verdächtige Zimmer
machtest du harmlos, aus deinem Herzen voll Zuflucht
mischtest du menschlichern Raum seinem Nacht-Raum hinzu.
Nicht in die Finsternis, nein, in dein näheres Dasein
hast du das Nachtlicht gestellt, und es schien wie aus Freundschaft.
Nirgends ein Knistern, das du nicht lächelnd erklärtest,
so als wüßtest du längst, *wann* sich die Diele benimmt . . .

The Third Elegy

It's one thing to sing the beloved. Something else, alas,
to sing the deeply hidden, guilty river-god of the blood.
Her young lover, whom she knows only from afar, what could he
know about the lord of desire who often, in solitude and loneliness
and before she could soothe him, and as though she didn't exist,
lifted up his godlike head out of unfathomable depths and
summoned the night to endlessly dissatisfied uproar.
Oh the blood of Neptune and his terrifying trident.
Oh the dark wind of his breast breathing out of a swirling shell.
Listen as the night empties itself in silence. You stars,
isn't it from you that the lover's delight in the face of the
beloved stems? Doesn't his deepest insight into
her pure features come from the pure constellations?

It wasn't you, alas, it wasn't his mother
who bent the arc of his brow to so much expectation.
Not for you, compassionate girl, not for you
did his lips curve into more fruitful expressions.
Do you really think that your silent entrance is so
unsettling, you who wander like the morning wind?
Sure, you terrified his heart; but still more ancient terrors
plunged into him with disquieting shock. Call
him . . . you can't quite call him back from his dark companion.
Of course, he *wants* to escape and he does; unburdened,
he lives in your sheltering heart and grasps and begins himself.
But did he begin himself, truly?
Mother, *you* made him small, it was you who began him;
he was new to you, over his fresh eyes you
bent the friendly world and warded off things unfamiliar.
Ah, where are those simpler years when your slender form
shielded him from the surging chaos in and around him?
You hid so much from him then; you made the suspicious room
at night seem harmless, out of the refuge of your heart
you mingled a more human space into the spaces of his night.
Not in the darkness, no, but in your closer presence
you placed the nightlight, and it shone out like true friendship.
There wasn't a creak you couldn't smilingly explain,
as though you knew just *when* the floor would crackle . . .

Und er horchte und linderte sich. So vieles vermochte
zärtlich dein Aufstehn; hinter den Schrank trat
hoch im Mantel sein Schicksal, und in die Falten des Vorhangs
paßte, die leicht sich verschob, seine unruhige Zukunft.

Und er selbst, wie er lag, der Erleichterte, unter
schläfernden Lidern deiner leichten Gestaltung
Süße lösend in den gekosteten Vorschlaf—:
schien ein Gehüteter . . . Aber *innen*: wer wehrte,
hinderte innen in ihm die Fluten der Herkunft?
Ach, da *war* keine Vorsicht im Schlafenden; schlafend,
aber träumend, aber in Fiebern: wie er sich ein-ließ.
Er, der Neue, Scheuende, wie er verstrickt war,
mit des innern Geschehns weiterschlagenden Ranken
schon zu Mustern verschlungen, zu würgendem Wachstum, zu tierhaft
jagenden Formen. Wie er sich hingab—. Liebte.
Liebte sein Inneres, seines Inneren Wildnis,
diesen Urwald in ihm, auf dessen stummem Gestürztsein
lichtgrün sein Herz stand. Liebte. Verließ es, ging die
eigenen Wurzeln hinaus in gewaltigen Ursprung,
wo seine kleine Geburt schon überlebt war. Liebend
stieg er hinab in das ältere Blut, in die Schluchten,
wo das Furchtbare lag, noch satt von den Vätern. Und jedes
Schreckliche kannte ihn, blinzelte, war wie verständigt.
Ja, das Entsetzliche lächelte . . . Selten
hast du so zärtlich gelächelt, Mutter. Wie sollte
er es nicht lieben, da es ihm lächelte. *Vor* dir
hat ers geliebt, denn, da du ihn trugst schon,
war es im Wasser gelöst, das den Keimenden leicht macht.

Siehe, wir lieben nicht, wie die Blumen, aus einem
einzigen Jahr; uns steigt, wo wir lieben,
unvordenklicher Saft in die Arme. O Mädchen,
dies: daß wir liebten *in* uns, nicht Eines, ein Künftiges, sondern
das zahllos Brauende; nicht ein einzelnes Kind,
sondern die Väter, die wie Trümmer Gebirgs
uns im Grunde beruhn; sondern das trockene Flußbett
einstiger Mütter—; sondern die ganze
lautlose Landschaft unter dem wolkigen oder
reinen Verhängnis—: *dies* kam dir, Mädchen, zuvor.

And he listened and was soothed. So overpowering
was your gentle presence; tall but eagerly cloaked,
his fate stepped behind the wardrobe, and his easily delayed and
restless future conformed itself to the folds of the curtain.

And he himself, as he lay there, unburdened, under
drowsy eyelids dissolving into the sweetness of your
gentle creation, into the foretaste of sleep—:
he *seemed* sheltered . . . But *within:* who could avert,
who divert the floods of origin welling up within him?
Ah, there *was* no caution in the sleeper; sleeping, yes, but
dreaming and feverish: how fitfully he abandoned himself.
At once new and trembling, how caught up he was,
entangled in the ever spreading tendrils of inner event
already twisting into patterns, into strangling growth, and prowling
bestial forms. How he surrendered—. And loved.
Loved his inwardness, his interior wilderness,
this primal forest within him, where among silent decay
his heart stood, light green. Loved. Left it behind, went
through his own roots and out into the powerful source,
where his little birth was already outlived. Lovingly
he descended into the ancient blood, into ravines,
where the horrible lay, still gorged on his fathers. And everything
terrible knew him, winked at him as an accomplice.
Yes, the dreadful smiled . . . Seldom
had you smiled so tenderly, mother. How could he
not love what smiled at him. He had loved it
long *before* you, for while you carried him within,
it was already dissolved in the water that makes the embryo light.

Look, we don't love, like the flowers do, in a single
year; when we love, an immemorial sap
flows up through our arms. Know *this*, dear girl:
that we loved *within* us, not just someone still to come, but a
measureless gathering, not one child only
but the fathers, too, resting in our depths
like mountain ruins; also the dry riverbeds
of former mothers—; and the entire
soundless landscape under a clouded or
pure destiny—; *this*, girl, came before you.

Und du selber, was weißt du—, du locktest
Vorzeit empor in dem Liebenden. Welche Gefühle
wühlten herauf aus entwandelten Wesen. Welche
Frauen haßten dich da. Was für finstere Männer
regtest du auf im Geäder des Jünglings? Tote
Kinder wollten zu dir . . . O leise, leise,
tu ein liebes vor ihm, ein verläßliches Tagwerk,—führ ihn
nah an den Garten heran, gieb ihm der Nächte
Übergewicht . . . . . .
                    Verhalt ihn. . . . . .

And you yourself, how could you know
what primal time you stirred up in your lover.
What feelings welled up from beings now gone.
What women hated you there. What sinister
Men you roused up in his young veins? Dead
children wanted you . . . Oh gently, gently,
perform for him with love some confident daily task,—lead him
close to the garden, and give him what outweighs
the night . . . . . .
                    Restrain him . . . . . .

Die vierte Elegie

O Bäume Lebens, o wann winterlich?
Wir sind nicht einig. Sind nicht wie die Zug-
vögel verständigt. Überholt und spät,
so drängen wir uns plötzlich Winden auf
und fallen ein auf teilnahmslosen Teich.
Blühn und verdorrn ist uns zugleich bewußt.
Und irgendwo gehn Löwen noch und wissen,
solang sie herrlich sind, von keiner Ohnmacht.

Uns aber, wo wir Eines meinen, ganz,
ist schon des andern Aufwand fühlbar. Feindschaft
ist uns das Nächste. Treten Liebende
nicht immerfort an Ränder, eins im andern,
die sich versprachen Weite, Jagd und Heimat.
    Da wird für eines Augenblickes Zeichnung
ein Grund von Gegenteil bereitet, mühsam,
daß wir sie sähen; denn man ist sehr deutlich
mit uns. Wir kennen den Kontur
des Fühlens nicht: nur, was ihn formt von außen.
    Wer saß nicht bang vor seines Herzens Vorhang?
Der schlug sich auf: die Szenerie war Abschied.
Leicht zu verstehen. Der bekannte Garten,
und schwankte leise: dann erst kam der Tänzer.
Nicht *der*. Genug! Und wenn er auch so leicht tut,
er ist verkleidet und er wird ein Bürger
und geht durch seine Küche in die Wohnung.
    Ich will nicht diese halbgefüllten Masken,
lieber die Puppe. Die ist voll. Ich will
den Balg aushalten und den Draht und ihr
Gesicht aus Aussehn. Hier. Ich bin davor.
Wenn auch die Lampen ausgehn, wenn mir auch
gesagt wird: Nichts mehr—, wenn auch von der Bühne
das Leere herkommt mit dem grauen Luftzug,
wenn auch von meinen stillen Vorfahrn keiner
mehr mit mir dasitzt, keine Frau, sogar
der Knabe nicht mehr mit dem braunen Schielaug:
Ich bleibe dennoch. Es giebt immer Zuschaun.

The Fourth Elegy

O trees of life, when are you wintering?
We aren't at one, are not like the birds migrating
knowingly. Overtaken and belated,
we force ourselves suddenly into the wind
and fall into an unresponsive lake.
We're aware of flowering and fading at once.
And somewhere lions still move about, and in
their majesty know nothing of weakness.

But we, fully intending one thing,
already feel the expense of another. Hostility
is closest to us. Don't lovers always
approach each other's borders, although
they promise distance, hunting, and home.
   Then for some hurried sketch a wide
background of contrast is painfully prepared
so that we see it; for this at least is clear to us.
We are unfamiliar with the contours
of our feeling: only what forms it from without.
   Who hasn't sat anxiously before his heart's
curtain? It rose: the scenery was farewell.
Easy to understand. The familiar garden,
and swaying softly: then the dancer came.
Not *him*. Enough! And even if he moves well,
he's costumed, and becomes a bourgeois
and enters his apartment through the kitchen.
   I don't want these half-stuffed masks,
rather the puppet. It's full. I will
endure the shell and the wire and the face
formed of surfaces. Here. I'm waiting.
Even if the lights go out, and someone
says to me: No more—, even if the emptiness
comes to me in gray drafts from the stage,
even if none of my silent ancestors will sit
by me any longer, not a woman, not
even the boy with the squinting brown eye:
I'll stay put. One can always watch.

Hab ich nicht recht? Du, der um mich so bitter
das Leben schmeckte, meines kostend, Vater,
den ersten trüben Aufguß meines Müssens,
da ich heranwuchs, immer wieder kostend
und, mit dem Nachgeschmack so fremder Zukunft
beschäftigt, prüftest mein beschlagnes Aufschaun,—
der du, mein Vater, seit du tot bist, oft
in meiner Hoffnung, innen in mir, Angst hast,
und Gleichmut, wie ihn Tote haben, Reiche
von Gleichmut, aufgiebst für mein bißchen Schicksal,
hab ich nicht recht? Und ihr, hab ich nicht recht,
die ihr mich liebtet für den kleinen Anfang
Liebe zu euch, von dem ich immer abkam,
weil mir der Raum in eurem Angesicht,
da ich ihn liebte, überging in Weltraum,
in dem ihr nicht mehr wart. . . . : wenn mir zumut ist,
zu warten vor der Puppenbühne, nein,
so völlig hinzuschaun, daß, um mein Schauen
am Ende aufzuwiegen, dort als Spieler
ein Engel hinmuß, der die Bälge hochreißt.
Engel und Puppe: dann ist endlich Schauspiel.
Dann kommt zusammen, was wir immerfort
entzwein, indem wir da sind. Dann ensteht
aus unsern Jahreszeiten erst der Umkreis
des ganzen Wandelns. Über uns hinüber
spielt dann der Engel. Sieh, die Sterbenden,
sollten sie nicht vermuten, wie voll Vorwand
das alles ist, was wir hier leisten. Alles
ist nicht es selbst. O Stunden in der Kindheit,
da hinter den Figuren mehr als nur
Vergangnes war und vor uns nicht die Zukunft.
Wir wuchsen freilich und wir drängten manchmal,
bald groß zu werden, denen halb zulieb,
die andres nicht mehr hatten, als das Großsein.
Und waren doch, in unserem Alleingehn,
mit Dauerndem vergnügt und standen da
im Zwischenraume zwischen Welt und Spielzeug,
an einer Stelle, die seit Anbeginn
gegründet war für einen reinen Vorgang.

Am I not right? You who found our life
so bitter, tasting of mine, you, father,
tasting again and again as I grew up
the first cloudy infusion of my Must
and taken by the aftertaste of so strange a future,
tested and tried my clouded upturned glance,—
you, father, who within my deepest hope,
so often since you died, felt anxious for me,
and serenely surrendered the realms of
serenity the dead call their own for my little fate,
am I not right? And you, am I not right, you
who loved me for the small beginning of
love for you from which I always turned
because the space in your faces, even as
I loved it, passed into that worldspace,
where you no longer were . . .: when I'm minded
to wait before the puppet stage, no, to
stare into it so intensely that finally an angel
must arrive there, a player to balance
my gaze and bring the empty skins to life.
Angel and puppet: a compelling play at last.
Then what we always divide by being here
comes together there. Then the entire
cycle of change finally emerges out
of our seasons. Then the angel plays
above and beyond us. Look, the dying
surely notice how full of pretense is all
that we accomplish here, where
nothing is itself. Oh hours in childhood,
when more than just the past was
behind each shape and before us no future.
We grew freely; but sometimes we pressed
to grow too soon, half for the sake of
those with nothing but their being grownup.
And yet, in going about things alone,
amused by what endures, we stood there
in the spaces interspersed between world and toy,
in a place which was from the very
beginning established for a pure event.

Wer zeigt ein Kind, so wie es steht? Wer stellt
es ins Gestirn und giebt das Maß des Abstands
ihm in die Hand? Wer macht den Kindertod
aus grauem Brot, das hart wird,—oder läßt
ihn drin im runden Mund, so wie den Gröps
von einem schönen Apfel? . . . . . . Mörder sind
leicht einzusehen. Aber dies: den Tod,
den ganzen Tod, noch *vor* dem Leben so
sanft zu enthalten und nicht bös zu sein,
ist unbeschreiblich.

Who shows a child as he truly is? Who places
him in his constellation and gives the measure
of distance in his hand? Who makes his death
out of gray bread hardening,—or leaves it there
inside his round mouth, so like the hard core
of a lovely apple? . . . . . Murderers are easy
to understand. But this: to contain death,
the whole of death, even *before* life's truly
begun, so gently and not to be driven mad,
is indescribable.

Die fünfte Elegie

Frau Hertha Koenig zugeeignet

Wer aber *sind* sie, sag mir, die Fahrenden, diese ein wenig
Flüchtigern noch als wir selbst, die dringend von früh an
wringt ein *wem, wem* zu Liebe
niemals zufriedener Wille? Sondern er wringt sie,
biegt sie, schlingt sie und schwingt sie,
wirft sie und fängt sie zurück; wie aus geölter,
glatterer Luft kommen sie nieder
auf dem verzehrten, von ihrem ewigen
Aufsprung dünneren Teppich, diesem verlorenen
Teppich im Weltall.
Aufgelegt wie ein Pflaster, als hätte der Vorstadt-
Himmel der Erde dort wehe getan.
                                        Und kaum dort,
aufrecht, da und gezeigt: des Dastehns
großer Anfangsbuchstab . . . , schon auch, die stärksten
Männer, rollt sie wieder, zum Scherz, der immer
kommende Griff, wie August der Starke bei Tisch
einen zinnenen Teller.

Ach und um diese
Mitte, die Rose des Zuschauns:
blüht und entblättert. Um diesen
Stampfer, den Stempel, den von dem eignen
blühenden Staub getroffnen, zur Scheinfrucht
wieder der Unlust befruchteten, ihrer
niemals bewußten,—glänzend mit dünnster
Oberfläche leicht scheinlächelnden Unlust.

Da: der welke, faltige Stemmer,
der alte, der nur noch trommelt,
eingegangen in seiner gewaltigen Haut, als hätte sie früher
zwei Männer enthalten, und einer
läge nun schon auf dem Kirchhof, und er überlebte den andern,
taub und manchmal ein wenig
wirr, in der verwitweten Haut

The Fifth Elegy

Dedicated to Frau Hertha Koenig

But tell me, who *are* they, these travelers, even more
fleeting than we ourselves are, who urgently from
early on are wrung (for whose pleasure?)
by an ever discontented will? But it wrings them,
bends them, twists them and swings them,
flings and catches them again; and they fall as
if through oiled and slippery air back
to the threadbare carpet, worn thin by their
endless leaping and landing, this carpet abandoned
and alone in the world.
Stretched out like a bandage, as if the suburban
sky had battered the earth there.
                            And hardly there,
upright, there and displayed: the
great initial letter of Duration . . . , but even the strongest
men are rolled up again, for a joke, by that ever
approaching grip, the way August the strong would
crush a tin plate at the table.

Ah, and around this
center, the rose of watching: blooms
and sheds its leaves. And around this
pestle, this pistil, surrounded by the pollen
of its own dust, blossoms again into the false
fruit of its own displeasure, always
without awareness,—shining with thinning
surface, an easy specious smiling discontent.

There: the withered, wrinkled lifter,
an old man only drumming now,
shriveled up in his powerful skin, as if it earlier contained
two men, and the other were now
lying already in the churchyard, and he's outlived the other,
deaf and sometimes just a little
confused in his widowed skin.

Aber der junge, der Mann, als wär er der Sohn eines Nackens
und einer Nonne: prall und strammig erfüllt
mit Muskeln und Einfalt.

Oh ihr,
die ein Leid, das noch kein war,
einst als Spielzeug bekam, in einer seiner
langen Genesungen . . . .

Du, der mit dem Aufschlag,
wie nur Früchte ihn kennen, unreif,
täglich hundertmal abfällt vom Baum der gemeinsam
erbauten Bewegung (der, rascher als Wasser, in wenig
Minuten Lenz, Sommer und Herbst hat)—
abfällt und anprallt ans Grab:
manchmal, in halber Pause, will dir ein liebes
Antlitz entstehn hinüber zu deiner selten
zärtlichen Mutter; doch an deinen Körper verliert sich,
der es flächig verbraucht, das schüchtern
kaum versuchte Gesicht . . . Und wieder
klatscht der Mann in die Hand zu dem Ansprung, und eh dir
jemals ein Schmerz deutlicher wird in der Nähe des immer
trabenden Herzens, kommt das Brennen der Fußsohln
ihm, seinem Ursprung, zuvor mit ein paar dir
rasch in die Augen gejagten leiblichen Tränen.
Und dennoch, blindlings,
das Lächeln . . . . .

Engel! o nimms, pflücks, das kleinblütige Heilkraut.
Schaff eine Vase, verwahrs! Stells unter jene, uns *noch* nicht
offenen Freuden; in lieblicher Urne
rühms mit blumiger schwungiger Aufschrift:
>*Subrisio Saltat.*<

    Du dann, Liebliche,
du, von den reizendsten Freuden
stumm Übersprungne. Vielleicht sind
deine Fransen glücklich für dich—,
oder über den jungen
prallen Brüsten die grüne metallene Seide
fühlt sich unendlich verwöhnt und entbehrt nichts.
Du,

But the young one, the man, as though he were the son of a
neck and a nun: tautly and tightly filled
with muscles and simplicity.

O you,
whom a pain still so small
once received as a toy in one of its
long convalescences . . . .

You who fall down with the
thud that only fruits unripened
know, a hundred times each day, from the tree of a mutually
built movement (rushing like water in a few minutes through
spring and summer and autumn)—
fall down hard on the grave:
sometimes during short pauses, a loving
look toward your seldom tender mother
wants to arise; then it quickly loses itself in your body,
whose surface devours it, that timid and
rarely tried expression . . . And then once
again the man is clapping his hands for the leap, and before
the pain becomes more clear near your perpetually racing
heart, the burning in the soles of your feet comes
to meet you before its own spring, chasing a pair
of watering tears into your still living eyes.
And yet, blindly,
the smile . . . . .

Angel! oh take it and pluck it, that small-flowered healing
herb. Make a vase and preserve it! Place it among those joys
still unopened to us; in a lovely urn
praise it with a flowery swirling inscription:
                              "Subrisio Saltat."

    Then you, dear one,
you whom the most charming joys
mutely overleapt. Perhaps your fringes
are happy enough for you—,
or over your young
firm breasts the green metallic silk
feels itself endlessly indulged and lacking nothing.
You,

immerfort anders auf alle des Gleichgewichts schwankende Waagen
hingelegte Marktfrucht des Gleichmuts,
öffentlich unter den Schultern.

Wo, o *wo* ist der Ort—ich trag ihn im Herzen—,
wo sie noch lange nicht *konnten*, noch von einander
abfieln, wie sich bespringende, nicht recht
paarige Tiere;—
wo die Gewichte noch schwer sind;
wo noch von ihren vergeblich
wirbelnden Stäben die Teller
torkeln . . . . .

Und plötzlich in diesem mühsamen Nirgends, plötzlich
die unsägliche Stelle, wo sich das reine Zuwenig
unbegreiflich verwandelt—, umspringt
in jenes leere Zuviel.
Wo die vielstellige Rechnung
zahlenlos aufgeht.

Plätze, o Platz in Paris, unendlicher Schauplatz,
wo die Modistin, *Madame Lamort*,
die ruhlosen Wege der Erde, endlose Bänder,
schlingt und windet und neue aus ihnen
Schleifen erfindet, Rüschen, Blumen, Kokarden, künstliche Früchte—, alle
unwahr gefärbt,—für die billigen
Winterhüte des Schicksals.
. . . .

Engel!: Es wäre ein Platz, den wir nicht wissen, und dorten,
auf unsäglichem Teppich, zeigten die Liebenden, die's hier
bis zum Können nie bringen, ihre kühnen
hohen Figuren des Herzschwungs,
ihre Türme aus Lust, ihre
längst, wo Boden nie war, nur an einander
lehnenden Leitern, bebend,—und *könntens*,
vor den Zuschauern rings, unzähligen lautlosen Toten:
    Würfen die dann ihre letzten, immer ersparten,
immer verborgenen, die wir nicht kennen, ewig
gültigen Münzen des Glücks vor das endlich
wahrhaft lächelnde Paar auf gestilltem
Teppich?

always laid out on the swaying scales of equipoise,
like the market fruit of serenity,
openly beneath the shoulders.

Oh *where* is the place—I carry it in my heart—,
where they still never *could*, where they still fell
apart from one another, like mating animals
poorly paired;—
where the weights are still heavy;
where from their vainly wobbling
sticks the plates still totter and
drop . . . . .

And suddenly in this laborious nowhere, suddenly
the unspeakable place, where the pure Too-little
incomprehensibly changes—, leaps around
into an empty Too-much.
Where the difficult calculation
sums up to nothing.

Squares, oh squares in Paris, endless showplace,
where the milliner, *Madame Lamort,*
twists and weaves the restless ways of earth,
endless ribbons, and from them designs
new bows, frills, flowers, rosettes, artificial fruits—, all
falsely hued,—for the cheap
winter hats of fate.
. . . .

Angel!: If there were a place unknown to us and there,
on an unsayable carpet, lovers displayed what they
cannot seem to accomplish here, the daring
high figures of their heart's leaping,
their spires of pleasure, their
ladders long leaning only on each other,
where there never was ground, trembling,—and
could before the ring of onlookers, the countless soundless dead:
    Would they then throw down their last, ever hoarded,
forever hidden, unknown to us, eternally valid coins
of happiness before the finally, truly
smiling pair on the gratified
carpet?

Die sechste Elegie

Feigenbaum, seit wie lange schon ists mir bedeutend,
wie du die Blüte beinah ganz überschlägst
und hinein in die zeitig entschlossene Frucht,
ungerühmt, drängst dein reines Geheimnis.
Wie der Fontäne Rohr treibt dein gebognes Gezweig
abwärts den Saft und hinan: und er springt aus dem Schlaf,
fast nicht erwachend, ins Glück seiner süßesten Leistung.
Sieh: wie der Gott in den Schwan.
                    . . . . . .Wir aber verweilen,
ach, uns rühmt es zu blühn, und ins verspätete Innre
unserer endlichen Frucht gehn wir verraten hinein.
Wenigen steigt so stark der Andrang des Handelns,
daß sie schon anstehn und glühn in der Fülle des Herzens,
wenn die Verführung zum Blühn wie gelinderte Nachtluft
ihnen die Jugend des Munds, ihnen die Lider berührt:
Helden vielleicht und den frühe Hinüberbestimmten,
denen der gärtnernde Tod anders die Adern verbiegt.
Diese stürzen dahin: dem eigenen Lächeln
sind sie voran, wie das Rossegespann in den milden
muldigen Bildern von Karnak dem siegenden König.

Wunderlich nah ist der Held doch den jugendlich Toten. Dauern
ficht ihn nicht an. Sein Aufgang ist Dasein; beständig
nimmt er sich fort und tritt ins veränderte Sternbild
seiner steten Gefahr. Dort fänden ihn wenige. Aber,
das uns finster verschweigt, das plötzlich begeisterte Schicksal
singt ihn hinein in den Sturm seiner aufrauschenden Welt.
Hör ich doch keinen wie *ihn*. Auf einmal durchgeht mich
mit der strömenden Luft sein verdunkelter Ton.

Dann, wie verbärg ich mich gern vor der Sehnsucht: O wär ich,
wär ich ein Knabe und dürft es noch werden und säße
in die künftigen Arme gestützt und läse von Simson,
wie seine Mutter erst nichts und dann alles gebar.

War er nicht Held schon in dir, o Mutter, begann nicht
dort schon, in dir, seine herrische Auswahl?
Tausende brauten im Schoß und wollten *er* sein,
aber sieh: er ergriff und ließ aus—, wählte und konnte.

The Sixth Elegy

Fig tree, how long it's been meaningful to me,
how you almost pass over the blossom
entirely and into the ripe, determined fruit,
unpraised, press your pure mystery.
Like the fountain pipe, your arching branches
drive the sap down and up: and it springs out of sleep,
hardly awake, into the bliss of its sweetest achievement.
Look: like the god into the swan.
                        . . . . . . But we linger, alas,
we who glory in blooming, and we enter the belated
core hidden within our final fruit already betrayed.
In a few the drive to action arises so powerfully that
they are already standing and glowing in fullness of heart,
when the temptation to bloom touches the youth of their
mouth, touches their eyelids, like gentle night air:
heroes perhaps, and those destined to depart early,
whose veins a gardening death twists differently.
These plunge ahead: they come before
their own smile, like the team of horses in the mild
hollowed reliefs of the conquering king at Karnak.

The hero is strangely close to those who died young. Duration
doesn't touch him. His rising is his being; he takes
off always, and rushes into the altered constellation
of his constant danger. Few find him there. But
hiding us darkly in silence and suddenly inspired, fate
sings him into the storm of his rushing, roaring world.
I hear no one like *him*. All of a sudden his dark song
passes through me with the streaming air.

How I'd then prefer to hide from this longing: Oh to be a boy once
again, a boy, that I might still become it and sit quietly
leaning on the arms of the future and read of Samson,
how his mother at first bore nothing, then everything.

Was he not hero already within you, mother, didn't his
powerful selection already begin there, in you?
Thousands brewed in the womb, wanting to be *him*,
but look: he seized and excluded—, chose and could.

Und wenn er Säulen zerstieß, so wars, da er ausbrach
aus der Welt deines Leibs in die engere Welt, wo er weiter
wählte und konnte. O Mütter der Helden, o Ursprung
reißender Ströme! Ihr Schluchten, in die sich
hoch von dem Herzrand, klagend,
schon die Mädchen gestürzt, künftig die Opfer dem Sohn.

Denn hinstürmte der Held durch Aufenthalte der Liebe,
jeder hob ihn hinaus, jeder ihn meinende Herzschlag,
abgewendet schon, stand er am Ende der Lächeln,—anders.

And if he destroyed pillars, it was when he broke out
of the world of your body into the narrower world, where he
chose further and could. O mothers of heroes, sources
of ravaging streams! You ravines into which
virgins have already plunged lamenting,
from the heart's high rim, future sacrifices to the son.

For when the hero stormed through love's stages,
each raised him up, each heartbeat meant for him,
already turned away, he stood at the end of smiles—altered.

Die siebente Elegie

Werbung nicht mehr, nicht Werbung, entwachsene Stimme,
sei deines Schreies Natur; zwar schrieest du rein wie der Vogel,
wenn ihn die Jahreszeit aufhebt, die steigende, beinah vergessend,
daß er ein kümmerndes Tier und nicht nur ein einzelnes Herz sei,
das sie ins Heitere wirft, in die innigen Himmel. Wie er, so
würbest du wohl, nicht minder—, daß, noch unsichtbar,
dich die Freundin erführ, die stille, in der eine Antwort
langsam erwacht und über dem Hören sich anwärmt,—
deinem erkühnten Gefühl die erglühte Gefühlin.

O und der Frühling begriffe—, da ist keine Stelle,
die nicht trüge den Ton der Verkündigung. Erst jenen kleinen
fragenden Auflaut, den, mit steigernder Stille,
weithin umschweigt ein reiner bejahender Tag.
Dann die Stufen hinan, Ruf-Stufen hinan, zum geträumten
Tempel der Zukunft—; dann den Triller, Fontäne,
die zu dem drängenden Strahl schon das Fallen zuvornimmt
im versprechlichen Spiel. . . . Und vor sich, den Sommer.

Nicht nur die Morgen alle des Sommers—, nicht nur
wie sie sich wandeln in Tag und strahlen vor Anfang.
Nicht nur die Tage, die zart sind um Blumen, und oben,
um die gestalteten Bäume, stark und gewaltig.
Nicht nur die Andacht dieser entfalteten Kräfte,
nicht nur die Wege, nicht nur die Wiesen im Abend,
nicht nur, nach spätem Gewitter, das atmende Klarsein,
nicht nur der nahende Schlaf und ein Ahnen, abends . . .
sondern die Nächte! Sondern die hohen, des Sommers,
Nächte, sondern die Sterne, die Sterne der Erde.
O einst tot sein und sie wissen unendlich,
alle die Sterne: denn wie, wie, wie sie vergessen!

Siehe, da rief ich die Liebende. Aber nicht *sie* nur
käme . . . Es kämen aus schwächlichen Gräbern
Mädchen und ständen . . . Denn, wie beschränk ich,
wie, den gerufenen Ruf? Die Versunkenen suchen
immer noch Erde.—Ihr Kinder, ein hiesig
einmal ergriffenes Ding gälte für viele.
Glaubt nicht, Schicksal sei mehr, als das Dichte der Kindheit;

The Seventh Elegy

Not wooing, no longer shall wooing, outgrowing voice,
be the nature of your cry; but cry out more purely like the bird,
when the season suddenly rising carries him away, almost forgetting
that he is a troubled sorrowing creature and not only one solitary heart
to be thrown into the cheering light and the intimate sky. Like him
should you be wooing, not less—, so that, still invisible,
a friend would sense you, the silent one in whom an answer
slowly awakens and whose hearing is gradually warmed,—
the glowing companion of your boldest feeling.

Oh and the spring understands—there isn't a space
that doesn't echo the tone of announcement. At first each small and
questioning note sounds with the rising silence
a muted complicity with a purely affirmative day.
Then up the stairs, up the stairs calling to the temple of the future
dwelling in dreams—; then the trill, like a fountain
that presses its uprising stream forward, already foreseeing its fall
in a promising play . . . . And still before itself lies the summer.

Not only the mornings of all summers—no, not only how
they transform themselves into day and shine before beginning.
Not only the days, so tender around their flowers, and hanging above
and around those shapely trees, strong and powerful.
Not only the devotion of these unfolding forces,
not only the paths, not only the meadows in evening,
not only, after late storms, the inhaled freshness,
not only approaching sleep and an evening intuition . . .
but equally the nights! But also all those lofty summer
nights, and their stars, the stars of the earth.
Oh to be dead and to know them finally,
all the stars: for how, how could we forget them!

Look: I called for the beloved. But *she* alone didn't
come . . . Girls came out of their fragile graves
and stood there . . . For how could I limit the call,
once I called out? The unripe ones always seem
to seek the earth.—Children, a single nearby
thing fully grasped but once means so much.
Don't believe that fate is more than the density of childhood;

wie überholtet ihr oft den Geliebten, atmend,
atmend nach seligem Lauf, auf nichts zu, ins Freie.

Hiersein ist herrlich. Ihr wußtet es, Mädchen, *ihr* auch,
die ihr scheinbar entbehrtet, versankt—, ihr, in den ärgsten
Gassen der Städte, Schwärende, oder dem Abfall
Offene. Denn eine Stunde war jeder, vielleicht nicht
ganz eine Stunde, ein mit den Maßen der Zeit kaum
Meßliches zwischen zwei Weilen—, da sie ein Dasein
hatte. Alles. Die Adern voll Dasein.
Nur, wir vergessen so leicht, was der lachende Nachbar
uns nicht bestätigt oder beneidet. Sichtbar
wollen wirs heben, wo doch das sichtbarste Glück uns
erst zu erkennen sich giebt, wenn wir es innen verwandeln.

Nirgends, Geliebte, wird Welt sein, als innen. Unser
Leben geht hin mit Verwandlung. Und immer geringer
schwindet das Außen. Wo einmal ein dauerndes Haus war,
schlägt sich erdachtes Gebild vor, quer, zu Erdenklichem
völlig gehörig, als ständ es noch ganz im Gehirne.
Weite Speicher der Kraft schafft sich der Zeitgeist, gestaltlos
wie der spannende Drang, den er aus allem gewinnt.
Tempel kennt er nicht mehr. Diese, des Herzens, Verschwendung
sparen wir heimlicher ein. Ja, wo noch eins übersteht,
ein einst gebetetes Ding, ein gedientes, gekenietes—,
hält es sich, so wie es ist, schon ins Unsichtbare hin.
Viele gewahrens nicht mehr, doch ohne den Vorteil,
daß sie's nun *innerlich* baun, mit Pfeilern und Statuen, größer!

Jede dumpfe Umkehr der Welt hat solche Enterbte,
denen das Frühere nicht und noch nicht das Nächste gehört.
Denn auch das Nächste ist weit für die Menschen. *Uns* soll
dies nicht verwirren; es stärke in uns die Bewahrung
der noch erkannten Gestalt.—Dies *stand* einmal unter Menschen,
mitten im Schicksal stands, im vernichtenden, mitten
im Nichtwissen-Wohin stand es, wie seiend, und bog
Sterne zu sich aus gesicherten Himmeln. Engel,
dir noch zeig ich es, *da!* in deinem Anschaun
steh es gerettet zuletzt, nun endlich aufrecht.
Säulen, Pylone, der Sphinx, das strebende Stemmen,
grau aus vergehender Stadt oder aus fremder, des Doms.

how often you overtook the beloved, breathing,
breathing after the blissful course, passing into freedom.

Being here is glorious. You knew it, girls, yes even *you* knew,
though you seemed to be so lost and perishing—, in the dirtiest
streets of the city, you festering ones, left exposed as
refuse. For each of you was for an hour, or perhaps not
even for an hour, at one with a true measure of time scarcely
measurable between two moments—, when you had a sense
of being. Everything. Your veins full of being.
Only we forget far too easily what our laughing neighbor
neither confirms for us nor envies. We want it to be
visible, although the most visible happiness only allows
itself to become familiar when we transform it within ourselves.

Nowhere, dear one, will a world be but within us. Our
life advances always in transformation. And what's out there
always becomes smaller. Where there was once an enduring house,
a thoughtful formation now suggests itself, belonging completely
to what's thinkable, as though it stood wholly within the brain.
Our era builds for itself vast storehouses of power, and formless
like the straining forces it wrests thrillingly from everything.
Temples are no longer known. We are the ones who secretly store up
these extravagances of the heart. Where one of them survives
still, a thing we used to pray to and worship and kneel before—,
it is already passing, just as it is, into the invisible realm within us.
Many no longer perceive it, and miss the fleeting opportunity
to build it once again *inside* themselves, with pillars and statues, greater!

Each torpid turning of the world has its disinherited ones,
to whom neither the earlier nor what's about to come truly belongs.
For even what lies very close is far away from humankind. But this
should not confuse *us*; it should strengthen in us a preserving of
the form we can still recognize.—This once *stood* among humankind,
stood in the midst of that annihilating destiny, it stood in the midst
of Not-Knowing-Whither, like something truly existing, and bent
the stars toward itself from the safety of heaven. Angel,
to *you* I will show it, *there*! in your infinite gaze
it will stand fully upright and saved at last.
Pillars, pylons, the Sphinx, the striving thrust
of the cathedral, gray, from a fading or strange city.

War es nicht Wunder? O staune, Engel, denn *wir* sinds,
wir, o du Großer, erzähls, daß wir solches vermochten, mein Atem
reicht für die Rühmung nicht aus. So haben wir dennoch
nicht die Räume versäumt, diese gewährenden, diese
unseren Räume. (Was müssen sie fürchterlich groß sein,
da sie Jahrtausende nicht unseres Fühlns überfülln.)
Aber ein Turm war groß, nicht wahr? O Engel, er war es,—
groß, auch noch neben dir? Chartres war groß—, und Musik
reichte noch weiter hinan und überstieg uns. Doch selbst nur
eine Liebende—, oh, allein am nächtlichen Fenster. . . .
reichte sie dir nicht ans Knie—?
                                        Glaub *nicht*, daß ich werbe.
Engel, und würb ich dich auch! Du kommst nicht. Denn mein
Anruf ist immer voll Hinweg; wider so starke
Strömung kannst du nicht schreiten. Wie ein gestreckter
Arm ist mein Rufen. Und seine zum Greifen
oben offene Hand bleibt vor dir
offen, wie Abwehr und Warnung,
Unfaßlicher, weitauf.

Was it not marvelous? Be astonished, Angel, for *we* are it,
we, O Great One; tell others that we were able to do this, my breath
doesn't reach far enough for praising. So we haven't failed
so far to put these spaces to use, the generous spaces, these
spaces of *ours*. (How terrifyingly great must these spaces be;
thousands of years haven't flooded them with our feelings.)
But a tower was great, was it not? O Angel, was it not great,—
even when it stood next to you? Chartres was great,—and music
reached still higher and passed even farther beyond us. But even
a woman in love—all alone at night near the window . . . .
did she not reach your knee—?
                      Don't think I'm wooing, Angel.
And even if I were wooing you, Angel, you wouldn't come. For my
call is always full of departure; and against such a strong
current you are unable to move. Like an outstretched arm
is my call. And its hand held open and reaching up
to grasp something remains open before you
as if in warning and defense,
far above the ungraspable.

Die achte Elegie

Rudolf Kassner zugeeignet

Mit allen Augen sieht die Kreatur
das Offene. Nur unsre Augen sind
wie umgekehrt und ganz um sie gestellt
als Fallen, rings um ihren freien Ausgang.
Was draußen *ist*, wir wissens aus des Tiers
Antlitz allein; denn schon das frühe Kind
wenden wir um und zwingens, daß es rückwärts
Gestaltung sehe, nicht das Offne, das
im Tiergesicht so tief ist. Frei von Tod.
Ihn sehen wir allein; das freie Tier
hat seinen Untergang stets hinter sich
und vor sich Gott, und wenn es geht, so gehts
in Ewigkeit, so wie die Brunnen gehen.
    Wir haben nie, nicht einen einzigen Tag,
den reinen Raum vor uns, in den die Blumen
unendlich aufgehn. Immer ist es Welt
und niemals Nirgends ohne Nicht: das Reine,
Unüberwachte, das man atmet und
unendlich *weiß* und nicht begehrt. Als Kind
verliert sich eins im Stilln an dies und wird
gerüttelt. Oder jener stirbt und *ists*.
Denn nah am Tod sieht man den Tod nicht mehr
und starrt *hinaus*, vielleicht mit großem Tierblick.
Liebende, wäre nicht der andre, der
die Sicht verstellt, sind nah daran und staunen . . .
Wie aus Versehn ist ihnen aufgetan
hinter dem andern . . . Aber über ihn
kommt keiner fort, und wieder wird ihm Welt.
Der Schöpfung immer zugewendet, sehn
wir nur auf ihr die Spiegelung des Frein,
von uns verdunkelt. Oder daß ein Tier,
ein stummes, aufschaut, ruhig durch uns durch.
Dieses heißt Schicksal: gegenüber sein
und nichts als das und immer gegenüber.

Wäre Bewußtheit unsrer Art in dem
sicheren Tier, das uns entgegenzieht

The Eighth Elegy

Dedicated to Rudolf Kassner

With all eyes the creature sees
the open. Only our eyes are
reversed and placed all around them
like traps, surrounding their free exit.
What *is* out there we only know from
the animal's face; for already we turn
the young child forcibly around, so glancing back
it sees only forms, not the open, so
deep in the animal's face. Free from death.
We alone see *death*; the free animal
has its perishing always behind itself
and God in front, and when it moves, it moves
in eternity, as wells and fountains move.

    We never have, not even for a single day,
that pure space before us, into which flowers open
themselves endlessly. There's always world
and never nowhere without the Not: that pure
undivided element which one breathes and
endlessly *knows* and does not desire. As children
lose themselves in stillness and are shaken back
in this. Or someone dies and now *is* it.
For drawing close to death one no longer sees death
and stares *beyond*, perhaps with an animal's vast gaze.
Lovers, were not another nearby, ever
blocking the view, are near to it and astonished . . .
As if by oversight it opens for them
behind each other . . . But neither moves past
the other, and once again there comes to be a world.
The creation is ever turning back, and we
see in it only the reflection of its free space,
darkening before us. Or that some animal,
mutely and serenely looks us through and through.
This is what destiny means: to be opposed
and nothing save this and opposed forever.

If the secure animal approaching us from
a different direction had our kind of

in anderer Richtung—, riß es uns herum
mit seinem Wandel. Doch sein Sein ist ihm
unendlich, ungefaßt und ohne Blick
auf seinen Zustand, rein, so wie sein Ausblick.
Und wo wir Zukunft sehn, dort sieht es Alles
und sich in Allem und geheilt für immer.

Und doch ist in dem wachsam warmen Tier
Gewicht und Sorge einer großen Schwermut.
Denn ihm auch haftet immer an, was uns
oft überwältigt,—die Erinnerung,
als sei schon einmal das, wonach man drängt,
näher gewesen, treuer und sein Anschluß
unendlich zärtlich. Hier ist alles Abstand,
und dort wars Atem. Nach der ersten Heimat
ist ihm die zweite zwitterig und windig.
    O Seligkeit der *kleinen* Kreatur,
die immer *bleibt* im Schoße, der sie austrug;
o Glück der Mücke, die noch *innen* hüpft,
selbst wenn sie Hochzeit hat: denn Schoß ist Alles.
Und sieh die halbe Sicherheit des Vogels,
der beinah beides weiß aus seinem Ursprung,
als wär er eine Seele der Etrusker,
aus einem Toten, den ein Raum empfing,
doch mit der ruhenden Figur als Deckel.
Und wie bestürzt ist eins, das fliegen muß
und stammt aus einem Schoß. Wie vor sich selbst
erschreckt, durchzuckts die Luft, wie wenn ein Sprung
durch eine Tasse geht. So reißt die Spur
der Fledermaus durchs Porzellan des Abends.

Und wir: Zuschauer, immer, überall,
dem allen zugewandt und nie hinaus!
Uns überfüllts. Wir ordnens. Es zerfällt.
Wir ordnens wieder und zerfallen selbst.

Wer hat uns also umgedreht, daß wir,
was wir auch tun, in jener Haltung sind
von einem, welcher fortgeht? Wie er auf
dem letzten Hügel, der ihm ganz sein Tal
noch einmal zeigt, sich wendet, anhält, weilt—,
so leben wir und nehmen immer Abschied.

consciousness—, it would tear us away
with its movement. But its being is for it
endless, unfathomable and without
regard for its state, and pure, like its gaze.
And where we see the future, it sees the All
and itself in the All and healed forever.

And still there is in the wakeful, warm animal
the weight and the concern of a great sadness.
For it also always bears the burden of what
often overwhelms us,—the recollection,
as if the place we are ever pressing toward was
once nearer and more true and its communion
infinitely tender. Here everything is distance,
and there it was breath. After that first home
the second one is ambiguous and windy.
    O the bliss of the *tiny* creature,
which *remains* always in the sheltering womb;
O joy of the gnat which still leaps within,
even when it has to marry: for everything is womb.
And look at the partial security of the bird,
which almost knows both from their source,
as if it were the soul of an Etruscan,
out of the dead one and received in a space,
but with its reclining figure serving as lid.
And how dismayed is the one who must fly
and who emerges from the womb. As if terrified
before itself and crossing through the air, the way a
crack runs through a cup. So the trace of a bat
quivers and tears through the porcelain of evening.

And we: spectators, always, and everywhere,
turned toward everything and never outward!
It overfills us. We arrange it. And it falls apart.
We arrange it once again and fall apart ourselves.

Who has twisted us around like this, so that,
no matter what we do, in each of our postures
we are always going away? Just as, upon the final
and farthest hill, which shows him his entire valley
one last time, he turns himself around, stops, lingers—,
so we live here, and are always taking leave.

Die neunte Elegie

Warum, wenn es angeht, also die Frist des Daseins
hinzubringen, als Lorbeer, ein wenig dunkler als alle
andere Grün, mit kleinen Wellen an jedem
Blattrand (wie eines Windes Lächeln)—: warum dann
Menschliches müssen—und, Schicksal vermeidend,
sich sehnen nach Schicksal? . . .

                    Oh, *nicht*, weil Glück *ist*,
dieser voreilige Vorteil eines nahen Verlusts.
Nicht aus Neugier, oder zur Übung des Herzens,
das auch im Lorbeer *wäre* . . . . .

Aber weil Hiersein viel ist, und weil uns scheinbar
alles das Hiesige braucht, dieses Schwindende, das
seltsam uns angeht. Uns, die Schwindendsten. *Ein* Mal
jedes, nur *ein* Mal. *Ein* Mal und nichtmehr. Und wir auch
ein Mal. Nie wieder. Aber dieses
ein Mal gewesen zu sein, wenn auch nur *ein* Mal:
irdisch gewesen zu sein, scheint nicht widerrufbar.

Und so drängen wir uns und wollen es leisten,
wollens enthalten in unsern einfachen Händen,
im überfüllteren Blick und im sprachlosen Herzen.
Wollen es werden.—Wem es geben? Am liebsten
alles behalten für immer . . . Ach, in den andern Bezug,
wehe, was nimmt man hinüber? Nicht das Anschaun, das hier
langsam erlernte, und kein hier Ereignetes. Keins.
Also die Schmerzen. Also vor allem das Schwersein,
also der Liebe lange Erfahrung,—also
lauter Unsägliches. Aber später,
unter den Sternen, was solls: *die* sind *besser* unsäglich.
Bringt doch der Wanderer auch vom Hange des Bergrands
nicht eine Hand voll Erde ins Tal, die Allen unsägliche, sondern
ein erworbenes Wort, reines, den gelben und blaun
Enzian. Sind wir vielleicht *hier*, um zu sagen: Haus,
Brücke, Brunnen, Tor, Krug, Obstbaum, Fenster,—
höchstens: Säule, Turm . . . . aber zu *sagen*, verstehs,
oh zu sagen *so*, wie selber die Dinge niemals
innig meinten zu sein. Ist nicht die heimliche List

The Ninth Elegy

Why, if this span of existence, when it reaches us, can
be brought forward as laurel, a bit darker than all other
green, with tiny waves on the edges of each
leaf (like the smile of a breeze)—: why then must we be
human beings—and, ever avoiding our destiny,
keep on longing for destiny? . . .

Oh *not* because happiness *is*,
that rashly snatched advantage in approaching loss.
Not out of curiosity, and not as practice for the heart,
which *would be* in the laurel too . . . . .

But because being here is so much, and because everything
local apparently needs us, all those fugitive things that
oddly penetrate us. Us, the most fugitive thing of all. *Once*
for each thing, and only *once. Once* and then no more. And we too
just *once*. Never again. But to have been
just *once* and even if only for *one* short season:
to have been this *earthly* seems to be irrevocable.

And so we press ahead and want to achieve it,
wanting to hold it firmly in our simple hands,
in the overflowing gaze and in the speechless heart.
Wanting to become it.—To whom does it give?
We'd hold it all forever . . . Ah, but what can one carry over,
alas, and into that other relation? Not the power of looking, that was
learned so slowly here, and nothing eventful here. Nothing.
The sufferings, then. And before everything the heaviness,
and the long experience of being in love,—just
what is wholly unsayable. But later,
among the stars, what yields: *they* are *better* unsayable.
For the wanderer brings from the mountain-slopes into
the valley, not some handful of earth, unsayable to all, but
a word he's gained, a pure word, the yellow and blue
gentian. Perhaps we are *here* in order to say: house,
bridge, fountain, gate, pitcher, fruit tree, window,—
at most: column and tower . . . . but to *say*, understand,
oh to say them *so* much more deeply than the things
themselves intended to be. Is it not the secret design of

dieser verschwiegenen Erde, wenn sie die Liebenden drängt,
daß sich in ihrem Gefühl jedes und jedes entzückt?
Schwelle: was ists für zwei
Liebende, daß sie die eigne ältere Schwelle der Tür
ein wenig verbrauchen, auch sie, nach den vielen vorher
und vor den Künftigen . . . . , leicht.

Hier ist des *Säglichen* Zeit, *hier* seine Heimat.
Sprich und bekenn. Mehr als je
fallen die Dinge dahin, die erlebbaren, denn,
was sie verdrängend ersetzt, ist ein Tun ohne Bild.
Tun unter Krusten, die willig zerspringen, sobald
innen das Handeln entwächst und sich anders begrenzt.
Zwischen den Hämmern besteht
unser Herz, wie die Zunge
zwischen den Zähnen, die doch,
dennoch, die preisende bleibt.

Preise dem Engel die Welt, nicht die unsägliche, *ihm*
kannst du nicht großtun mit herrlich Erfühltem; im Weltall,
wo er fühlender fühlt, bist du ein Neuling. Drum zeig
ihm das Einfache, das, von Geschlecht zu Geschlechtern gestaltet,
als ein Unsriges lebt, neben der Hand und im Blick.
Sag ihm die Dinge. Er wird staunender stehn; wie du standest
bei dem Seiler in Rom, oder beim Töpfer am Nil.
Zeig ihm, wie glücklich ein Ding sein kann, wie schuldlos und unser,
wie selbst das klagende Leid rein zur Gestalt sich entschließt,
dient als ein Ding, oder stirbt in ein Ding—, und jenseits
selig der Geige entgeht.—Und diese, von Hingang
lebenden Dinge verstehn, daß du sie rühmst; vergänglich,
traun sie ein Rettendes uns, den Vergänglichsten, zu.
Wollen, wir sollen sie ganz im unsichtbarn Herzen verwandeln
in—o unendlich—in uns! Wer wir am Ende auch seien.

Erde, ist es nicht dies, was du willst: *unsichtbar*
in uns erstehn?—Ist es dein Traum nicht,
einmal unsichtbar zu sein?—Erde! unsichtbar!
Was, wenn Verwandlung nicht, ist dein drängender Auftrag?
Erde, du liebe, ich will. Oh glaub, es bedürfte
nicht deiner Frühlinge mehr, mich dir zu gewinnen—, *einer,*
ach, ein einziger ist schon dem Blute zu viel.

this darkly reticent earth, when it presses its lovers forward,
that within their feeling each thing may tremble with joy?
Threshold: what it is for two
lovers to be wearing down a little the old threshold of
their door, they too, after the many who came before them
and before the coming ones . . . , lightly.

Here is the time for the *sayable, here* is its homeland.
Speak and proclaim. More than ever
the things we can experience are vanishing, and
what pushes them aside is an act without an image.
An act beneath a crust, easily shattered as soon as
activity within outgrows it and seeks for itself new limits.
Our heart survives between the
hammers, like the tongue
between the teeth, and still, it
somehow remains praising.

Praise the world to the angel, not the unsayable one,
you cannot impress *him* with glorious feelings; in the universe
where he feels more feelingly, you are a novice. So show
him some simple thing, formed from generation to generation,
which lives as our own, close to hand and in our sight.
Speak to him of things. He will stand amazed, as you once did
by the rope-maker in Rome or the potter near the Nile.
Show him how happy a thing can be, and how innocent and ours,
how even lamenting grief resolves purely to form itself,
serves as a thing, or dies into a thing—and blissfully
escapes beyond the violin. And these things, which
live by perishing, understand that you praise them; fleeting,
they long for us to save them, us, the most fleeting of all.
They want us to transform them wholly, in the invisible heart,
within, oh endlessly within us! Whoever we may finally be.

Earth, isn't this what you want: to arise within us,
invisible?—Is this not your dream,
to be for once invisible?—Earth! invisible!
What is your urgent commission if not transformation?
Earth, dear one, I will. Oh believe me, your
springs are no longer needed to win me over,—*just one,*
a single one, is already too much for my blood.

Namenlos bin ich zu dir entschlossen, von weit her.
Immer warst du im Recht, und dein heiliger Einfall
ist der vertrauliche Tod.

Siehe, ich lebe. Woraus? Weder Kindheit noch Zukunft
werden weniger. . . . . Überzähliges Dasein
entspringt mir im Herzen.

From now on I am namelessly resolved for you.
You were always right, and your holiest insight
is our intimate death.

Look, I am living. On what? Neither childhood nor
future shrinks . . . . . Overflowing being
springs forth in my heart.

Die zehnte Elegie

Daß ich dereinst, an dem Ausgang der grimmigen Einsicht,
Jubel und Ruhm aufsinge zustimmenden Engeln.
Daß von den klar geschlagenen Hämmern des Herzens
keiner versage an weichen, zweifelnden oder
reißenden Saiten. Daß mich mein strömendes Antlitz
glänzender mache; daß das unscheinbare Weinen
blühe. O wie werdet ihr dann, Nächte, mir lieb sein,
gehärmte. Daß ich euch knieender nicht, untröstliche Schwestern,
hinnahm, nicht in euer gelöstes
Haar mich gelöster ergab. Wir, Vergeuder der Schmerzen.
Wie wir sie absehn voraus, in die traurige Dauer,
ob sie nicht enden vielleicht. Sie aber sind ja
unser winterwähriges Laub, unser dunkeles Sinngrün,
eine der Zeiten des heimlichen Jahres—, nicht nur
Zeit—, sind Stelle, Siedelung, Lager, Boden, Wohnort.

Freilich, wehe, wie fremd sind die Gassen der Leid-Stadt,
wo in der falschen, aus Übertönung gemachten
Stille, stark, aus der Gußform des Leeren der Ausguß
prahlt: der vergoldete Lärm, das platzende Denkmal.
O, wie spurlos zerträte ein Engel ihnen den Trostmarkt,
den die Kirche begrenzt, ihre fertig gekaufte:
reinlich und zu und enttäuscht wie ein Postamt am Sonntag.
Draußen aber kräuseln sich immer die Ränder von Jahrmarkt.
Schaukeln der Freiheit! Taucher und Gaukler des Eifers!
Und des behübschten Glücks figürliche Schießstatt,
wo es zappelt von Ziel und sich blechern benimmt,
wenn ein Geschickterer trifft. Von Beifall zu Zufall
taumelt er weiter; denn Buden jeglicher Neugier
werben, trommeln und plärrn. Für Erwachsene aber
ist noch besonders zu sehn, wie das Geld sich vermehrt, anatomisch,
nicht nur Belustigung nur: der Geschlechtsteil des Gelds,
alles, das Ganze, der Vorgang—, das unterrichtet und macht
fruchtbar . . . .
. . . . Oh aber gleich darüber hinaus,
hinter der letzten Planke, beklebt mit Plakaten des >Todlos<,
jenes bitteren Biers, das den Trinkenden süß scheint,
wenn sie immer dazu frische Zerstreuungen kaun . . . ,
gleich im Rücken der Planke, gleich dahinter, ists *wirklich*.

The Tenth Elegy

Someday, emerging from this furious insight, may I
sing out jubilation and praise to assenting angels.
Let not the clearly struck hammer of my heart be
garbled by some slackened, or hesitant, or
tattered string. Let my streaming countenance be
more luminous; let my invisible weeping rise up
and bloom. How dear you'll be to me then, you
anguished nights. Strange that I didn't kneel more deeply to
you, unconsoling sisters, and get lost
in your loosened hair. We, the ones who waste our pains.
How we glance beyond them, into woeful duration,
perhaps hoping for an end. But they truly are
our preserving winter leaves, our dark sense of green,
one season of the familiar year   , not only a stretch
of time—, but place, settlement, camp, soil and dwelling.

Alas, how strange, of course, are the streets in the city of grief,
where, in the false silence made up of drowning tones,
the form cast from the very wastepipe of emptiness loudly
boasts: the gilded to-do, and the tawdry memorial.
How entirely an angel would stamp out their soothing market,
bounded by the church and its bill of sale:
clean and pure but disappointing like a post office on Sunday.
But out there the borders are always rippling with the carnival.
The swings of freedom! Those divers and jugglers of zeal!
The quaint happiness of the marksman's shapely target,
which wriggles from the aim and makes metallic sounds
when the more skillful strikes. From applause to chance
he stumbles further; for booths with every curiosity
advertise, drum, and howl. But for grownups only there
is still something special to see, how money's increased, anatomically,
not for entertainment merely: the genitalia of money, the
process, the whole thing, everything—, this educates and makes
us fruitful . . . .
. . . . Oh, but a little farther beyond,
beyond the last billboard, plastered with posters for "Deathless,"
that bitter beer which seems so sweet to its drinkers,
when they're always chewing fresh distractions with it . . . ,
just in the back of the billboard, just behind it, things are *real*.

Kinder spielen, und Liebende halten einander,—abseits,
ernst, im ärmlichen Gras, und Hunde haben Natur.
Weiter noch zieht es den Jüngling; vielleicht, daß er eine junge
Klage liebt. . . . . . Hinter ihr her kommt er in Wiesen. Sie sagt:
—Weit. Wir wohnen dort draußen . . . .
                                          Wo? Und der Jüngling
folgt. Ihn rührt ihre Haltung. Die Schulter, der Hals—, vielleicht
ist sie von herrlicher Herkunft. Aber er läßt sie, kehrt um,
wendet sich, winkt . . . Was solls? Sie ist eine Klage.

Nur die jungen Toten, im ersten Zustand
zeitlosen Gleichmuts, dem der Entwöhnung,
folgen ihr liebend. Mädchen
wartet sie ab und befreundet sie. Zeigt ihnen leise,
was sie an sich hat. Perlen des Leids und die feinen
Schleier der Duldung.—Mit Jünglingen geht sie
schweigend.

Aber dort, wo sie wohnen, im Tal, der Älteren eine, der Klagen,
nimmt sich des Jünglinges an, wenn er fragt:—Wir waren,
sagt sie, ein Großes Geschlecht, einmal, wir Klagen. Die Väter
trieben den Bergbau dort in dem großen Gebirg; bei Menschen
findest du manchmal ein Stück geschliffenes Ur-Leid
oder, aus altem Vulkan, schlackig versteinerten Zorn.
Ja, das stammte von dort. Einst waren wir reich.—

Und sie leitet ihn leicht durch die weite Landschaft der Klagen,
zeigt ihm die Säulen der Tempel oder die Trümmer
jener Burgen, von wo Klage-Fürsten das Land
einstens weise beherrscht. Zeigt ihm die hohen
Tränenbäume und Felder blühender Wehmut,
(Lebendige kennen sie nur als sanftes Blattwerk);
zeigt ihm die Tiere der Trauer, weidend,—und manchmal
schreckt ein Vogel und zieht, flach ihnen fliegend durchs Aufschaun,
weithin das schriftliche Bild seines vereinsamten Schreis.—
Abends führt sie ihn hin zu den Gräbern der Alten
aus dem Klage-Geschlecht, den Sibyllen und Warn-Herrn.
Naht aber Nacht, so wandeln sie leiser, und bald
mondet empor, das über Alles
wachende Grab-Mal. Brüderlich jenem am Nil,
der erhabene Sphinx—: der verschwiegenen Kammer
Antlitz.

Children play, and lovers hold each other,—in the distance,
solemnly in the sparse grass, and dogs do what's natural.
The young man is drawn still farther on; perhaps he is in love with
a young Lament . . . . . . He trails behind her into the meadows. She
says: it's far. We dwell out there . . . .
                              Where? And the youth
follows. Her bearing touches him. The shoulders, the neck,—maybe
she is of noble descent. But he leaves her behind, turns around,
looks back, waves . . . Why should I? She is a Lament.

Only those who died young, in the first state
of timeless equanimity, while still in weaning,
follow her lovingly. She waits
for maidens and befriends them. She shows them,
tenderly, what she has on. Pearls of grief and the fine
veils of patience.—With young men she treads in
silence.

But there, in the valley where they dwell, one of the elder Laments
responds to the youth when he questions:—We Laments,
she says, were once a powerful race. Our forefathers labored
in the mines up there, in the great mountain range; sometimes
you discover among men a piece of polished primal grief
or a slag of petrified fury from some ancient volcano.
Yes, that came from up there. We used to be rich.—

And she leads him gently through the vast landscape of Lament,
shows him the pillars of the temples or the rubble of
each castle where, long ago, the princes of Lament
ruled the land wisely. Shows him the towering
trees of tears and the fields of blossoming grief,
(the living only know it now as gentle shrubbery);
shows him the grieving animals, grazing,—and sometimes
a bird is terrified and, flying low through their upturned glance,
traces far away the written image of its solitary cry.—
At night she leads him out to the graves of elders,
the sibyls and prophets among the race of Laments.
But night draws near, they move softly, and soon
the gravestone rises up moonlike
to watch over all things. Like a brother to the one
by the Nile, the lofty Sphinx—: the reticent chamber's
countenance.

Und sie staunen dem krönlichen Haupt, das für immer,
schweigend, der Menschen Gesicht
auf die Waage der Sterne gelegt.

Nicht erfaßt es sein Blick, im Frühtod
schwindelnd. Aber ihr Schaun,
hinter dem Pschent-Rand hervor, scheucht es die Eule. Und sie,
streifend im langsamen Abstrich die Wange entlang,
jene der reifesten Rundung,
zeichnet weich das neue
Totengehör, über ein doppelt
aufgeschlagenes Blatt, den unbeschreiblichen Umriß.

Und höher, die Sterne. Neue. Die Sterne des Leidlands.
Langsam nennt sie die Klage:—Hier,
siehe: den *Reiter*, den *Stab*, und das vollere Sternbild
nennen sie: *Fruchtkranz*. Dann, weiter, dem Pol zu:
Wiege; Weg; Das Brennende Buch; Puppe; Fenster.
Aber im südlichen Himmel, rein wie im Innern
einer gesegneten Hand, das klar erglänzende >*M*<,
das die Mütter bedeutet . . . . . .—

Doch der Tote muß fort, und schweigend bringt ihn die ältere
Klage bis an die Talschlucht,
wo es schimmert im Mondschein:
die Quelle der Freude. In Ehrfurcht
nennt sie sie, sagt:—Bei den Menschen
ist sie ein tragender Strom.—

Stehn am Fuß des Gebirgs.
Und da umarmt sie ihn, weinend.

Einsam steigt er dahin, in die Berge des Ur-Leids.
Und nicht einmal sein Schritt klingt aus dem tonlosen Los.

                                   *

Aber erweckten sie uns, die unendlich Toten, ein Gleichnis,
siehe, sie zeigten vielleicht auf die Kätzchen der leeren
Hasel, die hängenden, oder
meinten den Regen, der fällt auf dunkles Erdreich im Frühjahr.—

And they are astonished by the royal head that has forever
placed the human face silently
upon the scale of the stars.

Giddy from an early death, his sight can't
grasp it. And yet her gaze
frightens an owl behind the rim of the crown. And the bird
brushes by the cheek with slow downstrokes,
the one with the ripest curve,
and sketches faintly in the newly
dead's hearing, as on a double
unfolded page, some indescribable outline.

And higher, the stars. The new stars in the land of grief.
Slowly the Lament names them:—Here,
look: the *Rider*, the *Staff*, and the fuller constellation she
names: *Garland of Fruit*. Then, further, toward the Pole:
Cradle; *Path*; *The Burning Book*; *Puppet*; *Window*.
But in the southern sky, pure as an inscription
on a favored hand, the clear and sparkling *M*,
that signifies Mothers . . . .—

But the dead one must advance, and silently the elder Lament brings
him close to the ravine,
where it shimmers in the moonlight:
the very source of joy. With reverence
she names it and says:—among humans
it is a supportive stream.—

At the foot of the mountain
range, she embraces him, weeping.

He ascends alone, up the mountains of primal grief.
And not once do his footsteps echo from his soundless lot.

*

But if the endlessly dead awakened in us a sign and symbol,
look, they'd point perhaps to the catkins hanging from
the empty hazels, or they'd
intend the rain, falling onto the earth's dark soil in springtime,—

Und wir, die an *steigendes* Glück
denken, empfänden die Rührung,
die uns beinah bestürzt,
wenn ein Glückliches *fällt*.

And we, who think of happiness
rising, would sense the emotion,
that almost dismays us,
when a happy thing *falls*.

NOTES

Introduction

1. G. W. F. Hegel, *Phenomenology of Spirit*, trans. A. V. Miller (Oxford: Oxford University Press, 1977), 1.

2. Julius A. Elias, *Plato's Defense of Poetry* (Albany: State University of New York Press, 1984), 2.

3. See, for instance, Martin Heidegger, "What Are Poets For?" in *Poetry, Language, Thought*, trans. Albert Hofstadter (New York: Harper and Row, 1971).

4. Friedrich Nietzsche, *Beyond Good and Evil*, trans. Walter Kaufmann (New York: Vintage, 1989), 13.

5. See Plato's *Protagoras*, 331c and 333c. For a well-known instance of Socrates's interest in persons and the accounts they render of themselves, beyond the detachable arguments particular individuals present or represent, see Nicias's remark in the *Laches*, 187e–188a

6. Rainer Maria Rilke, *Sonnets to Orpheus: A New English Version, with a Philosophical Introduction*, trans. Rick Anthony Furtak (Scranton, Pa.: University of Scranton Press, 2007), 16.

7. We should also observe here that the Latin root (*ordo*) and its cognates are, as Nagy puts it, "connected to the metaphorical world of weaving, and each is preoccupied with the idea of beginnings," and that the language of order has played an important role in Latin poetry, comparable to the Greek notion of the *prooimion* (from *oimê*, thread), which begins the act of weaving (Gregory Nagy, *Plato's Rhapsody and Homer's Music* [Cambridge, Mass.: Harvard University Press, 2002], 80). The idea of order is, then, closely tied to certain conceptions of the work of poetizing. Whether Rilke himself had such thoughts in mind is, of course, impossible to say.

8. Mark Harman, "Introduction" to his translation of Rilke's *Letters to a Young Poet* (Cambridge, Mass.: Harvard University Press, 2011), 15.

9. There is more to be said about Kant's view, as I note in an essay I presented at the Pacific meeting of the American Philosophical Association in 2007, but that is another story than the one I'm trying to tell here, and one more consistent with the view I'm trying to support in what follows.

10. Much of Robert Pippin's Hegelian-inspired interpretations of art mean, I think, to show that Hegel was both right about the decline of art in a sense that Plato, to judge from the dialogues, would probably have appreciated; but that art of some sort may possibly survive the decline of art as a revelation of the divine. See, for instance, Pippin's most recent book *After the Beautiful* (Chicago: University of Chicago Press, 2014).

11. John T. Lysaker, *You Must Change Your Life: Poetry, Philosophy, and the Birth of Sense* (University Park: Pennsylvania State University Press, 2002), 29.

12. See Heidegger's discussion of symbol and metaphor in, for instance, the lecture course on "The Ister."

13. Plato, *Republic*, 401b–402a.

14. See, for instance, Martha Nussbaum's discussion of Proust in *Upheavals of Thought* (Cambridge, Eng.: Cambridge University Press, 2001). For criticism of Nussbaum's reading, consistent with some of my own views, see Joshua Landy's *Philosophy as Fiction: Self, Deception, and Knowledge in Proust* (Oxford: Oxford University Press, 2004).

15. There are, to be sure, poets and novelists who defend the author's right to dictate to readers and critics or, less aggressively, to decide with supreme authority, what the work means—Milan Kundera stands out (see *The Art of the Novel*)—but others, like Thomas Mann, who are happy to discover a meaning and an import in the interpretation and criticism of their work that wasn't a part of their conscious design.

16. For a recent attempt to defend the position that Plato was himself a Platonist, see Lloyd P. Gerson's *From Plato to Platonism* (Ithaca, N.Y.: Cornell University Press, 2013). His work is a meticulous study of the dialogues and an important stretch of the history of their interpretation, and I've learned a great deal from it. But I think Gerson is often guilty of not taking the literary form and the poetic resources of the Platonic dialogue as seriously as they ought to be taken.

Prelude

1. Keats to his brother, December 21, 1817.

2. Harman, "Introduction" to Rilke's *Letters to a Young Poet*, 1.

3. See Judith Jarvis Thomson, "More on the Metaphysics of Harm," *Philosophy and Phenomenological Research* 82, no. 2 (March 2011): 435–58. Thomson's discussion was presented at a meeting in Boulder, Colorado, in the summer of 2009.

4. Ralph Waldo Emerson, *Representative Men* (Cambridge, Mass.: Harvard University Press, 1996), 109.

Chapter One. An Ancient Quarrel between Philosophy and Poetry

1. The conversation with Ion provides a detailed example of what Socrates tells more generally about his dissatisfaction with the poets in Plato's *Apology*.

2. Iris Murdoch, "The Fire and the Sun," in *Existentialists and Mystics* (New York: Penguin, 1997), 393.

3. Plato, *Ion*, 530d.

4. Socrates observes that the rhapsode must not only learn the lines of Homer but "his thought" as well. "For one could never become a good rhapsode without understanding what the poet says: the rhapsode must interpret the poet's thought to his audience, and it's impossible to do that well without knowing what the poet means" (*Ion*, 530c).

5. Plato, *Republic*, 600d.

6. Plato, *Ion*, 530a.

7. As Allan Bloom notes in an essay on the dialogue, "Socrates . . . exposes the important kinds of human souls and their characteristic errors. To make this particular discussion a worthwhile enterprise for him, the empty reciter of Homer's poems must represent something beyond himself" (Bloom, "An Interpretation of Plato's *Ion*," in *Giants and Dwarfs* [New York: Touchstone, 1990], 138). The limits of Homeric epic are revealed throughout the dialogue, if only

between the lines. As Murdoch observes, the *Ion* offers something like a trial run of views developed at greater length in the *Republic* (Murdoch, "The Fire and the Sun," 392).

8. *Protagoras*, 347c. I agree with Asmis, that in the *Ion*, as well as the *Gorgias*, Socrates is not prepared to attack "the most respected of all poets, Homer, directly. Instead, he attacks theatrical productions and infers that all poetry plays to the crowd" (Elizabeth Asmis, "Plato on Poetic Creativity," in *The Cambridge Companion to Plato*, ed. Richard Kraut [Cambridge, Eng.: Cambridge University Press, 1992], 344).

9. Plato, *Ion*, 534b.

10. Penelope Murray provides a short but insightful account of the history and pre-history of Plato's conception of poetic inspiration in *Plato on Poetry* (Cambridge, Eng.: Cambridge University Press, 1996). See especially 6–12 and 24–28.

11. An excerpt is included in *Selected Prose of T. S. Eliot*, ed. Frank Kermode (New York: Farrar, Straus and Giroux, 1975). Eliot shares, however, Socrates's suspicion that appeals to inspiration may lead us to overestimate the worth of some poetry: "The faith in mystical inspiration is responsible for the exaggerated repute of *Kubla Khan*" (90). But in an excerpt from an essay on Pascal, Eliot observes, commenting upon the religious thinker's conversion experience and its relation to his philosophical and literary work, "You may call it communion with the Divine, or you may call it a temporary crystallization of the mind. Until science can teach us to reproduce such phenomena at will, science cannot claim to have explained them; and they can be judged only by their fruits" (238).

12. In her own account of the quarrel between the poet and the philosopher, Susan B. Levin has argued persuasively that the attack upon poetry in Plato's dialogues challenges the poet's work in light of its failure to achieve the status of an art or science (*technê*). See Levin, *The Ancient Quarrel between Philosophy and Poetry Revisited: Plato and the Greek Literary Tradition* (Oxford: Oxford University Press, 2001). Her work is unique, as far as I know, in locating a Platonic engagement with, and criticism of, the poets in the *Cratylus*, which most commentators have interpreted as a response to the views of certain pre-Platonic philosophers and contemporary sophists.

13. Plato, *Ion*, 538c.

14. Collingwood argues in *The Principles of Art* (Oxford: Oxford University Press, 1958) that Plato thought poetry a *technê* of sorts. For a dissenting opinion, see Levin's *The Ancient Quarrel*, chapter 5. Penelope Murray reminds us that the conception of the poet as a craftsman, as well as an inspired being, goes back a long way: "Already in the *Odyssey* (17.382–5) the bard is described as a *demioergos*, a worker who is prized for his technical skill, and there are frequent references to the poet's expertise in early Greek poetry, expressed by terms such as *oida, epistemai, sophos* and *sophia*" (*Plato on Poetry*, 8) As she goes on to claim, Plato appears to diverge most significantly from his predecessors in holding that inspiration and technical expertise are incompatible.

15. Plato, *Ion*, 542b.

16. There are too many instances in the dialogues to track, where one or more of Socrates's interlocutors appeal to the poetic dictum to support, without argument, a controversial claim (the cultured elite in the *Republic* come readily to mind); and Socrates more or less consistently deflates the appeal to poetry, in

favor of the more discursive approach to the topics at hand, often by way of asking, first, what the poet might have meant in saying what he did.

17. This view finds expression in the discussion of musical education in books 2 and 3 of the *Republic*.

18. See Plato, *Republic*, X, especially 604a–605c.

19. Bloom, "An Interpretation of Plato's *Ion*," 155.

20. To be more precise, we should speak of Plato's opposition to *mimetic* poetry (epic, tragedy, comedy, and the like); for the philosopher is himself a sort of poet (or maker) who copies the eternal patterns and archetypes of all things in thought and, if he assumes political power, creates a just social order by copying the form of the good, and embodying it, as far as possible, in the real world of human affairs. In the *Laws*, Plato even suggests that the lawmaker is a sort of imitator, for the true polis is an imitation of the best and noblest life. The tragic poet and the statesman are rivals and antagonists, then, in the noblest of dramas. The mimetic theory of poetry has a long history; and if Abrams is right, it was the primary way of discussing art until the rise of Romanticism in Germany and England, as mind came to be seen in an active and creative light, and poetry came to be viewed as an outpouring or expression of intense feeling. But most of the theorists in this tradition cut against the grain of Platonism in finding, with Aristotle, nobility and value in the mimetic arts. What Plato found most disturbing, that the mimetic poet has all creation as his object—"all the plants that grow from the earth, and . . . all the animals, including himself; and . . . earth and sky and gods and everything in the sky, and everything in Hades beneath the earth" [*Republic, 596c*]—constituted, for theorists like Richard Hurd, the very dignity of the poet's calling.

21. Plato, *Republic*, X, 607b. Eric Havelock's *Preface to Plato* (Cambridge, Mass.: Harvard University Press, 1982) remains among the best accounts of Plato's attack on the poets, in the context of ancient Greek culture and the Homeric tradition.

22. The task of criticism, according to Wellek and Warren in their influential *Theory of Literature*, is to deal with the poem as poem. This could be seen as a twentieth-century version of the nineteenth-century movement of *l'art pour l'art*: the end of a poem is not to instruct or to edify or to mean anything beyond itself, but merely to *be*. In some varieties, more at home, perhaps, among French theorists, inspired by Saussure and Jakobson, criticism comes into its own when it brackets the quest for meaning and reference altogether, in favor of questions concerning *how* poems and novels mean: "the perception of the literary dimensions of language is largely obscured if one submits uncritically to the authority of reference" (Paul de Man, *Allegories of Reading: Figural Language in Rousseau, Nietzsche, Rilke, and Proust* [New Haven, Conn.: Yale University Press, 1979], 5). But later in the same work, de Man notes (in connection with Rilke) that the very idea of a language "entirely freed of referential constraints is properly inconceivable" (49). We cannot, it seems, bracket reference altogether, even if we only mean reference to the ordinary uses and meanings of words, still in detachment from the world, or experience, or what you will.

23. Recall the three beds in *Republic* X: the one in nature, manufactured by the god, the many of use brought into being by the craftsman, and the mere appearance of a bed created by the painter, "third from king and truth" (597e).

24. Imitation affects an inferior part of the soul, not the best (*beltiston*), and so is "an inferior thing that consorts with another inferior thing to produce an inferior offspring" (603b). Poetry's power to corrupt by nurturing those passions and appetites that ought to be dried up is, Socrates insists, "our chief charge against imitation" (605c).

25. See Shelley's "In Defense of Poetry."

26. Herodotus, *The History*, II.52.

27. Pippin, *After the Beautiful*, 7.

28. Christopher Janaway, *Images of Excellence: Plato and the Critique of the Arts* (Oxford: Oxford University Press, 1995), 4.

29. "In contrast [to the ancients], for us today, the beautiful is the relaxing, what is restful and so intended for enjoyment. Art then belongs in the domain of the pastry chef" (Martin Heidegger, *Introduction to Metaphysics*, trans. G. Fried and R. Polt [New Haven, Conn.: Yale University Press, 2000], 140).

30. For a non-fanatical critique of purely aesthetic values, see Wayne Booth's *The Company We Keep*.

31. Plato's banishment of the mimetic poets from Kallipolis finds, perhaps, its fiercest recent echo in the writings of Bentham, for whom poetry and truth are in natural opposition and (scientific) truth fatal to poetry. At best, poetry provides a privileged class with certain *amusements*; but as Bentham famously declared, in defense of the idea of pursuing the greatest happiness of the greatest number, poetry is less valuable than the pushpin. For a helpful discussion of the utilitarian attack on poetry, see M. H. Abrams's *The Mirror and the Lamp* (Oxford: Oxford University Press, 1953), 300–303. Nietzsche's anti-utilitarian quip, perhaps unfair, is at least worth quoting, if only for its humor: "Man does *not* strive for pleasure; only the Englishman does" (*Twilight of the Idols* [New York: Penguin Books, 1990], "Maxims and Arrows," aphorism 12).

32. Plato was, of course, opposed on this point by Aristotle, who argued in the *Poetics* that poetic statements are more philosophical than their historical counterparts because more *universal*: the historian tells us what happened in the singular, the poet what *might* occur; the domain of poetry is the possible.

33. To be sure, many still look to sacred texts for certain *ultimate* truths about the nature of the soul, what, if anything, comes after death, where salvation is to be sought, and so on. And in some respects, the quality of these texts could be defined as poetic. But with the exception of certain biblical literalists, few of us read, say, the story of creation in Genesis as an actual account of the beginning of the cosmos, and better than the empirical scientist's theories. And those who do deny that the account(s) are in any sense *poetic*—intelligent design theorists try to defend their credibility precisely by maintaining the *scientific* value of their work. To classify a text as poetic is almost tantamount to calling it untrue.

34. There were attempts in the seventeenth century to make room for the poetic expression of the truth of scientific (Newtonian) theory, but poetry was viewed largely as a didactic affair, in the service of making science more attractive and accessible to the layman. And the voice of skepticism soon followed. See, again, Abrams's *The Mirror and the Lamp*, 303–12.

35. As E. R. Dodds made the point, or reinforced the prejudice, in a famous essay on *Oedipus Rex*, "I wish undergraduates would stop writing essays which begin with the words 'This play *proves* that . . .' Surely no work of art can ever

'prove' anything: what value would there be in a 'proof' whose premises are manufactured by the artist" (Dodds, "On Misunderstanding the *Oedipus Rex*," reprinted in Harold Bloom's *Modern Critical Interpretations: Sophocles' Oedipus Rex*, 44). William Gass, writing on Rilke, observes (smugly) that the *Elegies* offer only "conclusions, not arguments, so—again—they cannot be philosophical." It is a mistake to "ennoble ideas that are made mostly of emotions, moods, and attitudes by calling them philosophical" (Gass, *Reading Rilke: Reflections on the Problems of Translation* [New York: Alfred A. Knopf, 2000], 110). But this apparently doesn't prevent the poet from having worked out "his epistemology," as Gass observes on p. 137, apparently forgetting what he'd said earlier.

36. The term "ontology" seems to have been coined by Johannes Clauberg in his *Elementa philosophiae sive Ontosophiae* (1647). I owe the reference to Jean-Luc Marion, who brought Clauberg to my attention in a seminar on Descartes at the University of Chicago.

37. I speak of "nature" in connection with Plato somewhat loosely. Although the *Republic* often invokes *phusis* as a standard of measure, the status of nature in Plato is certainly contestable; and given the theory of forms, or at least one possible interpretation of it, the source of the good we find in nature stands on the other side of the physical world, and according to a provocative claim in the sixth book beyond even being itself. And if Heidegger is right, the Greeks know nothing of what we call value, which suggests an act of preference, or the subject's endowing something with significance.

38. The metaphysics and theory of knowledge sketched out in the *Republic* are the outgrowth of an attempt to determine the nature of *justice* and the good life, as if to say: the ontological task is to articulate what the world and our knowledge of it must be like, if a certain form of life is to be shown to be possible.

39. Shelley, in fact, makes his own the view of poetic composition as a matter of inspiration presented by Socrates in the middle stretch of the *Ion* (533c–536d). We should also mention Walter Pater, the English aesthete (see his essays on the Renaissance) who published an interesting book on *Plato and Platonism*, and Santayana, the well known, if often ignored, American philosopher who wrote important studies on poetry and aesthetics, and a neglected work on *Platonism and the Spiritual Life*. Gerson is probably right to observe that it is Schleiermacher "who is the true originator of the idea that the philosophy [of Plato] is inseparable from the literary form of the dialogues (*From Plato to Platonism*, 83, footnote 23)

40. For an illuminating account of German Romanticism's relation to Plato, with special emphasis upon the importance of artistic form for philosophy, see the first chapter of Rüdiger Bubner's *The Innovations of Idealism* (Cambridge, Eng.: Cambridge University Press, 2003). Manfred Baum has argued convincingly that Schelling's most original philosophical project—namely, the *Naturphilosophie*—owes a great deal to Plato, especially the *Timaeus*. See his "The Beginnings of Schelling's Philosophy of Nature" in *The Reception of Kant's Critical Philosophy: Fichte, Schelling, and Hegel*, ed. Sally Sedgwick (Cambridge, Eng.: Cambridge University Press, 2007).

41. For what it's worth, I'm inclined to agree with Alexander Nehamas that Plato's attacks on poetry, mediated by Socrates in the dialogues, reflects a political and moral worry, "a specific social and historical gesture" anchored in the

uses of poetry in the fifth century, and should not be interpreted as an attack upon poetry as such. (See Nehamas, "Plato and the Mass Media," in *Plato on Art and Beauty* [New York: Palgrave Macmillan, 2012].)

42. M. F. Burnyeat, "Art and Mimesis in Plato's *Republic*," in *Plato on Art and Beauty*, 54. Levin defends a similar view in *The Quarrel*, 150–67.

43. As Christopher Janaway tersely observes, commenting upon the passage in question, "Plato uses 'literary' means to 'induce much thought' here. Abandoning the clipped dialogue style, he emulates the flow of poetry's language and its profusion of images" (Janaway, *Images of Excellence: Plato's Critique of the Arts*, 20).

44. See, for instance, Stanley Rosen's discussion of book 10 in his commentary on Plato's *Republic* and Elizabeth Asmis's chapter on Plato and poetic creativity in *The Cambridge Companion to Plato*.

45. Plato, *Laws*, 817a–d.

46. G. M. A. Grube, *Plato's Thought* (Indianapolis: Hackett, 1980), 179.

47. Grube suggests, on the basis of chronological considerations, combined with the tone and style he purports to discover in works alleged to be late, that Plato himself at last "grew impatient of his own art" (*Plato's Thought*, 207). This may be true, but it doesn't detract from the artfulness of the *Protagoras*, the *Symposium*, and the *Phaedrus*, to take three of Grube's own examples.

48. Christopher Rowe's impressive work on *Plato and the Art of Philosophical Writing* usefully, and, I think, in fairness to what Plato intended to achieve by way of the dialogue form, focuses on Plato's artful efforts to *persuade* his readers; that is, its "first concern is with understanding the nature of Platonic *rhetoric*" (Rowe, *Plato and the Art of Philosophical Writing* [Cambridge, Eng.: Cambridge University Press, 2007], vii). Rowe is sensitive to the overwhelming variety of Plato's art, and the chorus of voices that appears throughout the dialogues, and often within one dialogue (the *Symposium* is paradigmatic in this regard).

49. F. Schlegel, *Kritische Ausgabe* I, 332 (quoted by Bubner in *The Innovations of Idealism*, 32).

50. Plato, *Meno*, 86b. The dialogue also contains one of the more pregnant poetic descriptions of Socrates's effect upon his conversation partners, which is "very like the stingray in the sea, which benumbs whatever it touches" (80a).

51. The expression is Nietzsche's (see *The Birth of Tragedy* [Cambridge, Eng.: Cambridge University Press, 1999]), 75 and 82. The source of Nietzsche's conception of a *musiktreibender Sokrates* is the brief account in Plato's *Phaedo* of a Socrates who adapted certain fables by Aesop and the hymn to Apollo in metrical form. Socrates tells his Pythagorean interlocutors that he wished to test the meaning of frequently recurring dreams urging him not to neglect the Muses, to "make music and work at it" (*Phaedo*, 60c–61b).

52. For an account of the Pythagorean influence on Plato, see Phillip Sidney Horky's *Plato and Pythagoreanism* (Oxford: Oxford University Press, 2013). For references to Orpheus in Plato's dialogues, see W. K. C. Guthrie's *Orpheus and Greek Religion* (Princeton, N.J.: Princeton University Press, 1993), 12.

53. Again, Gerson: "In addition to the basic literary form of Plato's writings, there are literary forms within the dialogues, including myth and rhetorical displays" (*From Plato to Platonism*, 83).

54. Plato, *Republic*, 506c.

55. Plato, *Republic*, 514a.

56. Plato, *Sophist*, 230c.

57. Plato, *Sophist*, 259e. This comes forward in a dialogue that means to distinguish the reality of the philosopher from the (spurious) image of the philosopher (the sophist), and that continues the Platonic attack upon images we find in dialogues like the *Republic*.

58. Plato, *Symposium*, 206b. I think that Leo Strauss is right to see the dialogue as a confrontation between philosophy and poetry (Socrates is surrounded in the dialogue by lovers of poetry, and his culminating speech [attributed to Diotima] comes directly *after* the speeches of the comedic poet Aristophanes and the tragic poet Agathon, and includes chiding remarks directed at both poets along the way); but, as Strauss himself is clearly aware, as his readings of Plato and several of his remarks show, this doesn't rule out the need for a poetic, or a literary, approach to the dialogue; in fact, the dialogue form appears to demand it. (See Leo Strauss, *On Plato's "Symposium"* [Chicago: University of Chicago Press, 2001].) And as Strauss himself observes, facing the dreary accounts of human nature and experience among the social scientists of the last century, "Poetry is the capstone of wisdom. Poetry alone makes for the most comprehensive knowledge." Further: "I don't question that social science analyses are very important, but still, if you want to get a broad and a deep view you read a novel rather than social science" (ibid., 7).

59. Plato, *Timaeus*, 29d.

60. Plato, *Phaedrus*, 246a–257a. An illuminating discussion of Socrates's appeal to myth in the dialogue can be found in Charles Griswold's *Self-Knowledge in Plato's "Phaedrus"* (University Park: Pennsylvania University Press, 1986), chapter 4.

61. In the *Gorgias* both the poet and the sophist are said to be adept at nothing more and nothing less than pandering to the crowd and gratifying the audience. Tragedy is said to aim at the pleasure, rather than the improvement, of the spectator (502b).

62. See my "Speaking Extravagantly: Philosophical Territory and Eccentricity in *Walden*," in *Thoreau's Importance for Philosophy*, ed. Rick Anthony Furtak, Jonathan Ellsworth, and James D. Reid (New York: Fordham University Press, 2012).

63. See Gerson's discussion of *hulê* in Plato and Aristotle in *From Plato to Platonism*, 79–80. Although Gerson does not discuss the importance of the poetic resources of the philosopher's discourse, I think that what he says about the fluidity of Plato's use of language and its codification in the Platonist tradition that subsequently emerges is at least consistent with the view I'm prepared to make my own about the complex relationship between experience, language, and philosophy.

64. In Ricoeur's fine phrase, captured in the title of his conclusion to *The Symbolism of Evil* (trans. Emerson Buchanan [New York: Beacon, 1969]), "the symbol gives rise to thought."

65. The Straussians have their own way of dealing with the problem (they deserve some credit for seeing it, at least); but I leave it to the reader to decide what to make of Socrates's depiction of the philosophic life and its virtues in ways that make it difficult to grasp how such a creature could be fit to rule.

66. Plato, *Symposium*, 215a–b.

67. G. R. F. Ferrari offers two readings of this central image in the *Phaedrus* that capture, in their opposition, the ambivalence of the philosopher's attitude toward poetry I'm suggesting here. In his book-length study of the *Phaedrus*, he reads the image of the cicadas as an emblem of the malady of being enchanted by the poetic statement; but in a more recent essay on the *Republic*, he opens with a retraction: "The cicadas' example of divine inspiration is positive" (Ferrari, "The Philosopher's Antidote," in *Plato on Art and Beauty*, 109). Whether one reads the myth of the cicadas as a critique of the poetic statement or as a positive account of the role poetry plays in the philosophic quest for truth about the most important (human) things, it matters above all that Socrates chooses to speak (ambivalently) about the nature of the philosophic life in *images* of excellence and debasement.

68. Plato, *Phaedrus*, 250d and 250c.

69. It is consequently baffling to read in Friedländer's book on Plato, in a hefty chapter devoted to myth, that "Socrates . . . is not a 'mythologist,' not a teller of stories" (*Plato: An Introduction*, trans. Hans Meyerhoff [New York: Harper, 1969], 172). He does, however, qualify the claim by noting that Plato himself created "the myth of Socrates." And in the long run, his account of the mythical elements in the dialogues is consistent with what I'm suggesting here.

70. Emmanuel Levinas, *Totality and Infinity*, trans. Alphonso Lingis (Pittsburgh: Duquesne University Press, 1969), 33.

Chapter Two. *Dichtung und Wahrheit*

1. See Harry G. Frankfurt, *The Importance of What We Care About* (Cambridge, Eng.: Cambridge University Press, 2005).

2. Heidegger takes most of the history of modern philosophy, including the work of the neo-Kantians and his teacher Husserl, to task for failing to place the phenomenon of care at the center of the philosophy of human existence. I discuss Heidegger's aversions, and their broader philosophical implications, in "Ethical Criticism in Heidegger's Early Freiburg Lectures," in the *Review of Metaphysics* 59(1): 33–71 (2005).

3. Friedrich Nietzsche, *The Will to Power*, trans. Walter Kaufmann and R. J. Hollingdale (New York: Vintage Books, 1968), note 1067.

4. As Heidegger notes in a lecture course on the philosophy of religion, the world is *not*, at least not initially, an object; for you cannot *live* in an object. The world is originally the place where human beings dwell; and we are *in* it *not* in the manner of a cup in a cupboard, but by way of being affected by what we care about, and being able to get around competently in our dealings with things (*pragmata*), and being touched by others. William James and John Dewey, and other pragmatists, would have agreed.

5. I develop this connection between being and the good in an unpublished essay on "Being and the Good in Early Heidegger: An Essay in Moral Ontology," presented at the Southwest Seminar in Continental Philosophy (Brigham Young University, June 2012), and throughout *Heidegger's Moral Individuals*.

6. The first division of *Sein und Zeit* remains the best argument for this thesis. But see also Husserl's late work on the *Lebenswelt* in, inter alia, *The Crisis*, and Merleau-Ponty's *Phenomenology of Perception*. We should also mention Goethe

in this context, and Heller's helpful discussion of the poet's quarrel with Newton in *The Disinherited Mind*.

7. Erich Heller, *The Disinherited Mind* (New York: Harcourt Brace, 1975), 272.

8. William Wordsworth, "Preface to the *Lyrical Ballads*," in *The Norton Anthology of English Literature*, vol. 2, ed. M. H. Abrams (New York: W. W. Norton & Co., 1993), 1439.

9. "Aristotle, I have been told, hath said, that poetry is the most philosophical of all writing; it is so: its object is truth, not individual and local, but general, and operative; not standing upon external testimony, but carried alive into the heart by passion; truth which is its own testimony, which gives strength and divinity to the tribunal to which it appeals, and receives them from the same tribunal. Poetry is the image of man and nature" (Wordsworth, "Preface to the *Lyrical Ballads*," 1444).

10. *The Disinherited Mind*, 272.

11. The list comes from the "Ninth Elegy."

12. In the English-speaking world, we have Stanley Cavell to thank for this insistence upon the philosophical problem of the ordinary, with the help of Wittgenstein and Austin, but also Heidegger. See, for instance, Cavell's *The Claim of Reason* (Cambridge, Mass.: Harvard University Press, 1999) and his *Conditions Handsome and Unhandsome* (Chicago: University of Chicago Press, 1990).

13. Iris Murdoch, *Existentialists and Mystics*, ed. Peter Conradi (New York: Penguin, 1997), 60

14. This view finds its way into Harry Frankfurt's *The Reasons of Love* (Princeton, N.J.: Princeton University Press, 2004).

15. J. L. Mackie, *Ethics: Inventing Right and Wrong* (New York: Penguin Books, 1990), 15.

16. Ibid., 18. The distinction between questions of fact and questions of value, worth, meaning, and significance holds even William James in grip. See, for instance, his *The Varieties of Religious Experience* (New York: Penguin Books, 1985), 4–5 and 150.

17. Recall Kant's subtle account of aesthetic judgments in the third *Critique*: the judgment of taste tells us nothing about the object but merely how we are affected by it. We find beautiful those things that arouse a free but harmonious play among our own cognitive powers.

18. *Ethics: Inventing Right and Wrong*, 34.

19. Hegel, too, is interested in the limits of external authority in ethical life and places freedom at the center of his views on the moral life; but unlike Mackie, Hegel's vision of a world in which freedom finds itself at home is rich and value-laden.

20. Kleist's despairing response to the *Critique of Pure Reason* comes to mind here, as Nietzsche reports it in "Schopenhauer as Educator" in *Untimely Meditations*, ed. Daniel Breazeale and trans. R. J. Hollingdale (Cambridge, Eng.: Cambridge University Press, 1997), 140–41.

Chapter Three. The Philosophical World of the *Duino Elegies*

1. On metamorphosis see Malraux's *The Voices of Silence* and my short unpublished essay on the topic "A Traditional Aspect of Malraux's Theory of Art: A Reply to Derek Allan."

2. To justify keeping explanatory notes to a minimum in his translation of the *Elegies*, Snow reminds us in a short "Preface" that Rilke "distrusted commentaries as dilutions and foreclosures of the individual's reading experience" (Rilke, *Duino Elegies*, trans. Edward Snow [New York: North Point, 2000], xii). This is true enough, and worth remembering. But it is also worth remembering that Rilke himself commented frequently upon his own work, if only in letters (a fact noted by Snow himself) *and* on the work of other artists, including Cézanne (in letters to Clara) and Rodin and the landscape painters at Worpswede (in published essays).

3. For a helpful account of the elegiac poetry in Germany, see Theodore Ziolkowski's *The Classical German Elegy 1795–1950* (Princeton, N.J.: Princeton University Press, 1980). In what follows, only a few of the strategies probed in the *Elegies* will be explored, in keeping with the modesty of our task. For a fuller account, see Kathleen Komar's essential work *Transcending Angels* (Lincoln: University of Nebraska Press, 1987).

4. "Happiness," as Rousseau notes, "is too constant a condition and man too mutable a being for the one to suit the other" (Rousseau, "Notes for the Reveries," in vol. 12 of the *Collected Writings of Rousseau*, ed. and trans. Christopher Kelly [Hanover: University Press of New England, 2006], 50).

5. The "Seventh Elegy," II.4. Translations of the *Elegies* in what follows are my own.

6. The "Tenth Elegy," IV.5. "The promise that the work contains is anything but facile" (de Man, *Allegories of Reading*, 23). This needs to be asserted against a tendency to render Rilke's vision precious and so, I think, unconvincing, which, unfortunately, sometimes mars translations of and commentaries upon his work, including some of the more sentimental but still compelling early verse. Barrows and Macy, for instance, end their (partial) translation of *The Book of Hours* with a stanza from "The Book of Monastic Life" because, in their own words, "it provides a simple and reverent closure for the whole work" (*Rilke's Book of Hours*, trans. Anita Barros and Joanna Macy [New York: Riverhead Books, 2005], 257). But the third and last book deals uncomfortably with poverty and death, and embodies the fructifying anxieties of Rilke's Paris years. In their notes, Rilke is said, inter alia, to reveal a capacity for tantric play (246), to affirm an intuitive knowledge of God, more complete in our dreams (244), and to place "the erotic in the service of the sacred" (247), although we aren't told what talk of "the sacred" might mean, and in what contexts it (the erotic) sets itself against the religious. They also sometimes omit lines (as in their translation of I.6) because they find them repetitive and, after all, "Rilke was writing these very quickly!" (243). Their work, in short, seems driven by a prior decision regarding what a great poet must have to say, in order to console us, often at the expense of what, more complexly, he actually says.

7. Again, the reader is referred to Cavell's work, in this context on varieties of skepticism. For a perceptive account of the problem of skepticism in Cavell and Thoreau, see Rick Anthony Furtak's "Skepticism and Perceptual Faith: Henry David Thoreau and Stanley Cavell on Seeing and Believing," *Transactions of the Charles Sanders Peirce Society* 43 (2007): 542–61.

8. The "Second Elegy," II.5–6 and III.1–3.

9. Quoted by Komar on p. 26 of *Transcending Angels*.

10. The train of thought I'm sketching out here is a compressed version of Martha Nussbaum's account of the transcending movement in *Love's Knowledge* (Oxford: Oxford University Press, 1992), and my own thoughts in a chapter on death in a book manuscript in progress on Heidegger, ethics, and ontology.

11. Wallace Stevens, "Sunday Morning," V.3–5. A few lines later, death "makes the willow shiver in the sun." In the second stanza the poet asks: "What is divinity if it can come / Only in silent shadows and in dreams?" Stevens is worth mentioning here because, like Rilke, he has a few things to say about angels and the quest, in art, for meaning. See also Wallace Stevens's *The Necessary Angel: Essays on Reality and the Imagination* (New York: Knopf, 1951).

12. Rainer Maria Rilke, "The Young Workman's Letter" (1922) in *Where Silence Reigns: Selected Prose*, trans. G. Craig Houston (New York: New Directions Books, 1978), 73.

13. On the whole, I find Stephen Spender's views on the angel of the *Elegies* convincing. See "Rilke and Eliot" in *Rilke: The Alchemy of Alienation* (Lawrence: Regents Press of Kansas, 1980). Kathleen Komar has offered a thorough reading of the *Elegies* as a gradual overcoming of the temptations of the angelic order in her fine study *Transcending Angels*.

14. Wim Wender's film *Der Himmel über Berlin* (misleadingly translated as *Wings of Desire* and recently released by the Criterion Collection), inspired in part by the angel of Rilke's *Elegies*, seems to me to get things right. It's a story of angelic boredom and dissatisfaction, and the desire to fall into the human realm, where things have meaning, seriousness, and weight.

15. "Praise the world to the angel," as the poet commands in the "Ninth Elegy."

16. As H. F. Peters observes in "Dolls and Angels," the poet's placement between the angel and the earth "caused the fierce tensions in his life" (*Rainer Maria Rilke: Masks and the Man* [Seattle: University of Washington Press, 1960], 130).

17. Another reminder: what's offered below is selective. The reader will miss, for instance, a discussion of the hero in the "Sixth Elegy," but also a careful reading of the "Fourth" and the "Tenth" elegies. I have little to say in what follows about those who die young, although the *Elegies* are fruitful sources for those interested in the topic of the injustice of an early death. And I take liberties with the order of the poems as well, plunging into the "Fifth" at first, clearly in medias res, risking the reader's dissatisfaction.

18. This is not to say that the *Elegies* offer a secular form of salvation, an interpretation Jacob Steiner warns us against in *Rilkes Duineser Elegien* (Bern, 1962); but the *Elegies* lose their point if the affirmative ambition is lost.

19. I mean Schopenhauer, of course. The reference is to section 59 of *The World as Will and Representation*, volume 1.

20. For references, see J. Hillis Miller, *The Disappearance of God: Five Nineteenth-Century Writers* (Urbana: University of Illinois Press, 200), 24–25. And for provocative offerings on themes broached here, see Miller's sequel *Poets of Reality: Six Twentieth-Century Writers* (Cambridge, Mass.: Harvard University Press, 1966).

21. Walter Benjamin, *Illuminations*, ed. Hannah Arendt (New York: Schocken Books, 1968), 189.

22. Charles Dickens, *Bleak House*, ed. N. Bradbury (New York: Penguin Books, 1996), chapter 1, p. 13.

23. Ralph Waldo Emerson, "Nature," in *The Essays: Second Series*, text established by Alfred R. Ferguson and Jean Ferguson Carr (Cambridge, Mass.: Harvard University Press, 1987), 318.

24. For a useful discussion of *Malte* and the city, see "Hamlet in Paris" in Peter's *Rainer Maria Rilke: Masks and the Man*.

25. Rainer Maria Rilke, *The Notebooks of Malte Laurids Brigge*, trans. Stephen Mitchell (New York: Vintage International, 1985), 9.

26. Ibid. 48.

27. Ibid., 7.

28. Ibid., 73.

29. Ibid., 4.

30. Those acquainted with Rilke's biography will know what this confession means. Those interested in Rilke's life, about which I've remained intentionally silent, should consider consulting Ralph Freedman's *Life of a Poet* and Donald Prater's *A Ringing Glass*.

31. *Rainer Maria Rilke and Lou Andreas-Salomé: The Correspondence*, trans. Edward Snow and Michael Winkler (New York: Norton, 2006), 50.

32. Lou Andreas-Salomé, *You Alone Are Real to Me: Remembering Rainer Maria Rilke*, trans. Angela von der Lippe (New York: BOA Editions, 2003), 50.

33. The *Neue Gedichte* represent Rilke's triumph over the sentimental tendencies of some of his earlier verse. They represent, in Heller's words, "the total absorption of the poet's self in the object of his contemplation" (Heller, *The Poet's Self and the Poem: Essays on Goethe, Nietzsche, Rilke and Thomas Mann* [London: Athlone, 1976], 62). The importance of the thing (*das Ding*) in Rilke persists into the *Elegies*, as we shall see, against the romantic tendency toward inwardness and the scornful retreat from actuality. And as Peters suggests, the *New Poems* signal the poet's reaching beyond the confines of Malte's despair (*Rainer Maria Rilke*, 81). See also Walter Strauss's fine essay on Rilke and Ponge in *Rilke: The Alchemy of Alienation*. For an account of *das Ding* in Martin Heidegger's development, see my entry on the topic in the *Heidegger Lexicon*, ed. Mark Wrathall (Cambridge, Eng.: Cambridge University Press, forthcoming).

34. Again, quoting Heller, "despite his two visits, Russia remained a dream. The reality was Paris, and Paris would not let go. Each time he returned to it it was a homecoming" (*The Poet's Self*, 56)

35. As Komar usefully notes, the carpet that catches the acrobats' fall "becomes a patch to cover the wound inflicted on the natural world by the encroaching, humanly devised spaces of cities and suburbs" (*Transcending Angels*, 92).

36. Rainer Maria Rilke, "Worpswede" (1902/03), in *Where Silence Reigns,*, tr. G. Craig Houston (New York: New Directions, 1978), 13.

37. Ibid., 11.

38. Ibid., 13.

39. Ibid., 9.

40. Henry David Thoreau, "Walking," in *Walden and Other Writings*, ed. Brooks Atkinson (New York: Modern Library, 2000), 644. Thoreau adds, in what reads like a wonderful parody of the Christian *Credo*, "I believe in the forest, and in the meadow, and in the night in which the corn grows." We should mention Rousseau in this connection as well. In *Reveries of the Solitary Walker*, on the topic of his interest in botany, he writes, "Trees, shrubs, and plants are the

attire and clothing of the earth. Nothing is so sad as the sight of a plain and bare
countryside which displays only stones, clay, and sand to the eyes. But enlivened
by nature and arrayed in its nuptial dress amidst brooks and the song of birds,
the earth, in the harmony of the three realms, offers man a spectacle filled with
life, interest, and charm—the only spectacle in the world of which his eyes and
his heart never weary" ("Seventh Walk," in *Collected Writings of Rousseau*, vol.
8, p. 59).

41. Landy, *Philosophy as Fiction: Self, Deception, and Knowledge in Proust*, 33.

42. We could add here passages on nature or wildness within from the "Third
Elegy," discussed below.

43. We might recall here Whitman's lines (section 32 of "Song of Myself" in
Leaves of Grass), quoted by Bertrand Russell in *The Conquest of Happiness*:

> I think I could turn and live with animals, they're so placid and
>   self-contain'd,
> I stand and look at them long and long.
> They do not sweat and whine about their condition,
> They do not lie awake in the dark and weep for their sins,
> They do not make me sick discussing their duty to God,
> Not one is dissatisfied, not one is demented with the mania of
>   owning things,
> Not one kneels to another, nor to his kind that lived thousands
>   of years ago,
> Not one is respectable or unhappy over the whole earth.

44. Rilke, "Worpswede" (1902/03) in *Where Silence Reigns*, 9.

45. Rousseau's description of ecstasy and abandonment in *Reveries* comes
close to what Rilke attributes to the animal in the "Eighth Elegy": "A sweet and
deep reverie takes possession of his senses then, and through a delightful intoxi-
cation he loses himself in the immensity of this beautiful system with which he
feels himself one. Then, all particular objects elude him; he sees and feels nothing
except in the whole" (Rousseau, *Collected Writings*, vol. 8, 59). It is, however,
worth noting that there is an escapist strain in Rousseau's account of surrender
to nature, which is foreign to the final reconciling vision of the *Elegies*.

46. Emerson, "Nature" in *The Essays*, 317.

47. Eric L. Santner, *On Creaturely Life: Rilke, Benjamin, Sebald* (Chicago:
University of Chicago Press, 2006). Heidegger's critique can be found in a course
of lectures on Parmenides.

48. Blanchot suggests, provocatively, that by the "Open" Rilke means nothing
less than the poem itself. See Maurice Blanchot, *The Space of Literature*, trans.
Ann Smock (Lincoln: University of Nebraska Press, 1982), 142.

49. Here I agree with John Lysaker, that love "marks another ground word
in Rilke's poetry," and one that places Heidegger's indictment of the poet as a
modern metaphysician of Cartesian consciousness and subjectivity in a dubious
light. See footnote 17 on p. 36 of *You Must Change Your Life*. I also think that
Lysaker, following Heidegger, is right to see Rilke as a poet striving to think "the
being of beings," for reasons that should be abundantly clear by now (ibid., 37).

50. Rilke, "Worpswede" (1902/03) in *Where Silence Reigns*, 10.

51. Ibid., 22.

52. Critics of Rilke's worldview are quick to pounce on his diatribes against love. Even those otherwise sympathetic to the poet's stance see some failing here. Shaw, for instance, claims (without argument and in the absence of a more detailed analysis of the relevant texts) that Rilke's "description of human love never reached any full understanding of the reciprocity which it usually implies" (Priscilla Washburn Shaw, *Rilke, Valéry and Yeats: The Domain of the Self* [New Jersey: Rutgers University Press, 1964], 43).

53. Ralph Freedman, *Life of a Poet: Rainer Maria Rilke* (Evanston, Ill.: Northwestern University Press, 1996), 290.

54. Rilke, *Letters to a Young Poet*, 55.

55. Ibid., 59.

56. Letter from Rilke to Emanuel von Bodman, 1901, in *Letters on Life*, ed. and trans. Ulrich Baer (New York: Modern Library, 2006), 36.

57. Robert Hass, "Looking for Rilke," in *The Selected Poetry of Rainer Maria Rilke*, ed. and trans. Stephen Mitchell (New York: Vintage International, 1989), xxxiii.

58. From the poem *Wendung*, composed in Paris in 1914. In Stephen Mitchell's translation: "Work of the eyes is done, now / go and do heart-work / on all the images imprisoned within you; for you / overpowered them: but even now you don't know them" (*The Selected Poetry of Rainer Maria Rilke*, 136)

59. Blanchot, *The Space of Literature*, 136.

60. Ibid., 139.

61. Michel Haar, *The Song of the Earth*, trans. R. Lilly (Bloomington: Indiana University Press, 1993), 121. For a sustained and thoughtful critique of Heidegger's approach to poetry and Rilke, see Véronique M. Fóti's *Heidegger and the Poets* (New Jersey: Humanities, 1992).

62. Both quotations are taken from *The Song of the Earth*, 126.

63. Ibid., 127.

64. It is tempting to read the inward turn in light of the Romantic disaffection with the real world, destined to disappoint, or as an extension of the Stoic's return to the "inner citadel," where the mind stands a better chance of gaining control. Heller, for instance, reads this move in light of the rejection of the Classical and the task of redeeming the world by internalizing it: "at the climax of the *Duino Elegies*, the poet . . . does indeed drive poetry out of its classical mind" (Erich Heller, *The Artist's Journey into the Interior and Other Essays* [New York: Random House, 1965], 148). It is pretty clear, at least to me, that Rilke is no Stoic, although we'll have to consider the matter a bit more carefully, in connection with Platonism (the Stoic's original), toward the end, fast approaching, of our meditation on the *Elegies*. Rilke's relation to Romanticism, on the other hand, would require elaborate work in its own right. We'd have to consider interpretations of Romanticism offered by, among others, Abrams, Harold Bloom, and, more recently, Charles Larmore, whose *The Romantic Legacy* (New York: Columbia University Press, 1996) has helped place the Romantic tradition in a respectable philosophical context. We'd also have to contend with Paul de Man's *Romanticism and Contemporary Criticism* (Baltimore: Johns Hopkins University Press, 1993), and a host of twentieth-century poets (especially Eliot), whose work could be said to unfold in relation to the Romantic tradition they seem bent on

opposing. And we'd have to say something about Hölderlin, whose work has influenced almost everyone, but especially the philosophers whose work bears most directly upon our interpretation of Rilke. I content myself, if not the reader, to move ahead, admittedly leaving quite a few important things behind and in the dark along the way.

65. Quoted on p. 12 of *Philosophy as Fiction*.

66. For the idea of the world better off lost, and made rather than discovered, see Richard Rorty's *Contingency, Irony, and Solidarity*. The works opposing Rorty on this score are too numerous to list.

67. Haar, *The Song of the Earth*, 124. Haar is as eager as I am to rescue Rilke's poetry from the Heideggerian stigma of subjectivism; and his reading of Rilke, like my own, builds upon several insights worked out most fully by . . . Heidegger himself. We could say that the mind is gifted with interiority, as Heidegger often likes to remind us (building upon Husserl's conception of intentionality), or that "the world is endowed with interiority" insofar as it is somehow expressible.

68. See Rick Anthony Furtak's "Introduction" to his recent translation of the *Sonnets to Orpheus* (Scranton, Pa.: University of Scranton Press, 2007), 12, with reference to John Lysaker's *You Must Change Your Life: Poetry, Philosophy, and the Birth of Sense*.

69. Landy, *Philosophy as Fiction*, 34. I'm not so convinced that the preservation of otherwise fleeting things is guaranteed in Proust's novel by what Landy calls "the extratemporal self which has the power to recall Lost Time," but that's less important here.

70. Gerson rightly speaks of the paradox in Plotinus "that matter, which is evil, does partake of the Good" (*From Plato to Platonism*, 250).

71. Janaway, *Images of Excellence*, 79.

72. Plato, *Symposium*, 203c–d.

73. Ibid., 211c–d.

74. Letter from Rilke to Lou Andreas-Salomé, August 8, 1903 (in *Letters on Life*, 154).

75. Shakespeare, the 19th Sonnet, lines 13–14. The 18th Sonnet is better known, and more clearly evinces this poetic hostility to time, and confidence that the poet's "eternal lines" outmatch the death of the persons who occasion them. But the 83rd Sonnet places the poet's achievement in another, less confident light. The concluding couplet of this more despairing poem, despairing, at least, as a commentary upon what the poet can achieve, runs: "There lives more life in one of your fair eyes / Than both your poets can in praise devise."

76. Rilke, *Letters on Life*, 154.

77. On this point, see Hegel's argument on (and against) sense-certainty in the *Phenomenology of Spirit*.

78. Rilke, *Letters on Life*, 125.

79. Letter from Rilke to Hulewicz, November 13, 1925, in *Letters on Life*, 23.

80. Rilke, *Sonnets to Orpheus*, 2.13, translated by Furtak.

81. Letter from Rilke to Maria von Thurn und Taxis, September 6, 1915, in *Letters on Life*, 60. It is hard to imagine Plato (or Socrates in the dialogues of Plato's middle and late periods) saying anything like this. The Socrates of the *Apology*, however, could have said it.

82. "But to acquire for ourselves the earthly means, to reach a certain completeness in our relations to the earth, to be here, ineffably, indescribably, breathlessly: would that not be the only way for us finally to be gathered into something greater than mere earthliness?" (letter from Rilke to Ilse Erdmann, October 9, 1915, in *Letters on Life*, 100).

INDEX OF NAMES

INDEX OF SUBJECTS

In this index, page numbers in italics refer to Rilke's *Duino Elegies*, so that interested readers may consult relevant occurrences of terms in the poetry that play a significant role in the interpretive chapters. The terms *philosophy* and *poetry* are conspicuously absent merely because they appear in some form on almost every page.